A PASSAGE TO INDIA

An inspiring true story of
overcoming obstacles, challenges and adversity.

ISBN: 1477575340
ISBN 13: 9781477575345
Library of Congress Control Number: 2012909950
CreateSpace
North Charleston, SC

Dedicated with love to My Mom Tara Parmar and my angels Ria, Ryan and Krishna.

You are always in our hearts and never forgotten.

May your stars forever shine brightly

xxx

About the author

Vinay Parmar is the founder of The Bounce-Back-Ability Academy, an inspirational speaker, coach and author who has shared his powerful personal story of overcoming adversity with hundreds of people. His unique insights and lessons in dealing with change, empower individuals to overcome setbacks, challenges and obstacles with greater confidence, energy and purpose.

To discover more about Vinay's services and training programmes please visit www.vinayparmar.co.uk.

You can connect with Vinay online via twitter @vinaythespeaker or you can join him on Facebook on his fan page www.facebook.com/vinaythespeaker

Contents

Foreword

"July 9th!" proclaimed the priest. The tone of his voice vibrated with a kind of authority and confidence that you just would not question. After months of meetings and consultations, changing dates and adjusting plans, finally we had an agreed date for our wedding.

Jem and I were thrilled that the date was set; finally, we could relax a little…well maybe not quite relax, as the big fat Indian wedding machine was set well and truly into motion and our big day was finally becoming a reality. We had our civil wedding service a few months earlier; but the Indian wedding was the real deal – the moment within our culture where we would truly become a married couple and begin our life as a family.

Everyone in our large, extended family was excited and looking forward to our big day. However, nobody could have possibly imagined just how 'big' that day would turn out to be! July 9th 2000 would change my life in ways that I could have never have imagined.

Have you ever had that experience when your life or some part of it just seems to be going the way it should?

Maybe after painstaking planning, blood sweat and tears you have finally got everything just the way you want…then WAMMO!, life throws you a curve ball, which changes everything.

Change can and will affect us all…how, when and where, is not always within our control. Sometimes it is just a mild irritation but other times it can paralyse us and stop us dead in our tracks, and as such, it can have the most profound impact on everything that you believe in.

Little did I realize how profound an impact July 9th would have on me, and the direction in which my life would take as a result.

As often is the case in our darkest times, we sometimes discover our brightest and most inspirational moments. In essence, the following chapters contain a story of inspiration – tales of woe – transformed my life from personal tragedy to that of prosperity and fulfilment. The journey that I have taken throughout my life has shown me that life is not about the hand that you are dealt, but how you play that hand. Things happen in life; yet, despite our most harrowing moments of despair, there is a world of hope.

Our resolve is put to the test at some time in our lives…A Passage to India was my first step towards a Utopian existence.

Chapter One – Made In England

I was born on 20th February 1975 in Harrow, Middlesex. My Dad, Dhiraj Parmar, and my Mom, Tara, were immigrants. My Dad arrived in England as a student and began working in a launderette in Shepherd's Bush, London, for the princely wage of seven pounds per week. It was not quite the life that he had envisaged when he left his hometown of Nakuru in Kenya, where his family had a successful business.

In 1973, my Dad embarked on a trip back home to India, to search for his bride. His endeavours to find his wife were those, which were customary to most young Indian men of that generation, and, while accompanied by his brother-in-law and his sister, my Dad went on what I can only describe as a 'tour'. As he went from village to village, he had several potential partners picked out for him, in the hope that he would select his bride. (During his visit, no meetings or conversation was ever to take place with potential partners – just an awkward viewing surrounded by family members.)

After several failed viewings, a fortuitous conversation led him to a village where he met Mom. My Dad tells me that he knew she was the one the very moment that he had laid eyes on her. She was the eldest daughter of a schoolteacher turned insurance agent, and a well-respected one at that. Within two weeks, they had married and ultimately arrived back in England to begin their new life together.

Initially, my parents shared a house with my grandfather and my Dad's youngest brother. With the wonderful news that I was on the way, my grandfather was elated at the prospect of being the first of his grandchildren through one of his sons. It was shortly after I was born that we moved to Birmingham, where my Dad and his eldest brother went into business together and opened a grocery store specialising in Indian pickles and spices. They did very well, serving the local Indian community and developed what most business gurus would describe as a loyal customer base.

In the years that followed, I welcomed my younger siblings. My younger brothers, Dipit and Ricky were born far enough apart not to be in each other's space, yet close enough that we all shared a strong family bond.

My Dad was a hard working person; he left home in the early hours of the morning to visit the wholesale markets and came home later after completing home deliveries. He was part of a generation who were driven by the same desire to educate their children so that they would not experience the same hardships as they did. My Mom worked on an assembly line, producing coils for electrical motors and would do all the overtime that was possible, before returning home to prepare a freshly cooked evening meal. My parents were motivated like most immigrants to provide a life for their children that they themselves were never fortunate enough to have. They wanted to ensure that their children would never struggle in life the same way that they had, and as such, our education was to play a key role. They had high aspirations for us all, and they did not want to see us doing hard labour throughout our lives, and therefore directed us towards professional careers. I say 'directed' rather than 'expected', as what I remember most from my childhood is that my parents encouraged all three of us to follow our own interests, and at no time do I ever recall them standing in the way of our dreams.

I had a great childhood; having an extended family certainly has its benefits, and spending each summer with my cousins was indeed great fun! In primary school, I grew up with the same set of friends and it was only natural that we ended up attending the same secondary school. It was around that time that the house we were living in was becoming smaller (as we grew older), and therefore my parents began looking for another, more suitable and spacious accommodation. The opportunity arose for them to move us to a property that was more up market; a leafy suburb called Hall Green. Unfortunately, for me that meant a change of schools; change is difficult at the best of times but in your teenage years, I think it is that much harder. I did not really want to change, but eventually, I guess my natural sense of adventure took over and I embraced the upheaval.

It was during my childhood years that I found it rather difficult to fit in. At school, I was not the most academically gifted student; I always found creative arts far more interesting and inspiring than algebra, the periodic table or even the Bunsen Burner! In those early years, I felt like I was torn between two worlds…two identities and therefore I did not really know who I was.

I cannot remember how I began to make new friends but my school reports appeared to suggest that I was good at forming relationships. I had several new friends who lived close to my new home, which meant that we were able to walk to school together. The majority of my friends were white and they seemed to accept me into their group. However, most of the Asian kids saw me as a 'coconut' – brown on the outside but white in the middle. I think they saw me as being disloyal by abandoning my culture, which was ironic as my parents were heavily involved in our Indian community, and furthermore, I was actively taking part in dance performances and cultural events. I felt that it was unfair of them to judge me that way; because I did not hang out with them on a regularly basis, it did not make me any less Indian.

My teenage life was full of internal conflict; I was constantly trying to find a home in both camps, while battling stereotypes and discovering my own self-worth. I was teased a lot, too, because of my prominent features – having a large nose and big ears! I also became the butt of jokes when one of the kids called at my house and my non-English speaking grandma answered. He came to school the following day making squawking sounds, which the others found hilarious and at my own expense. I tried to laugh it off, however, inside it was killing me – not only because he was making fun of my family – it was beginning of the hate and turmoil that I felt within myself. Sometimes I wished that I just looked like everyone else, so that I would just fit in; but then I would see the richness of my culture through the activities that I was involved in, which filled me with a sense of pride.

Despite all that, I began to do well at school and big things were expected of me. I was far from the brightest kid in the school; however, I think that I was certainly 'punching above my weight'. My parents were optimistic for me, too. My Mom dreamt that I would become a doctor, solicitor, accountant or amount to a success in another profession of good standing and esteem within our community.

It was eventually through sport that I began to discover my sense of belonging. I tried football, but it was apparent that I was never going to make it beyond the school playground. I was actually a bit of a laughing stock; my goalkeeping was of the comedy variety. Cricket changed my life!

A local Sunday league team was looking to set up a youth team, and so my friends convinced me to go along for the trials. I made it through – I could not believe it – I was an occasional cricketer at that point. It was, however, with some coaching and encouragement that I began to improve. In fact, it was my first experience of someone other than my parents actually believing in my ability. John Snipe and Alf Rose at Earlswood Cricket Club took a raw, enthusiastic youngster and turned him into a half-decent bowler. I began to put in good performances for the club, and then the opportunity presented itself for me to play in the school team. Up until that point, I was a bit of a part player, yet some of the other players for the school were also with Earlswood. I cannot recall whom we were playing at that time, but I remember Jim, our ginger-haired skipper throwing me the ball.

The nerves had started to kick in and my heart was racing from the adrenalin. "Come on, Vin, you can do this. Just what you do for Earlswood," he said, calmly.

I marked my run up, polished the red leather of the ball on my crisp whites, and then started my approach. I was in flow. Everything was fluid and, as I delivered my first ball on target, it was greeted with applause and words of encouragement. I ended up taking two crucial wickets and suddenly I had arrived. My PE teacher and the rest of the team were proud of me, and I was the man…at least for a while anyway.

It appeared that I had hit a gold streak, not just on the field but also at school, as I felt more and more confident in my ability. I was hooked on the feeling; it was like a drug addiction. Cricket became a passion of mine and I would spend every spare moment (and many that were not spare) playing, practicing and enjoying the sport. However, my ongoing passion for the sport would eventually prove to be my undoing, and ultimately my studies were to suffer as a result. When I should have been revising for my GCSEs and concentrating on my career, I was in the nets – it showed in my exam results when they turned out to be disastrous – I flunked everything.

Dreams of a high-powered career disappeared in front of me. Not only that, but I was about to become the black sheep of the family. I could not understand how life could be so unforgiving – great one minute – bad the next. How would I face my parents? It was my first taste of real failure; sure, I had had some disappointments in the past, but this was an altogether different feeling. It would not be my last; yet, it most definitely played a key part in shaping me into the man that I am today.

My parents were obviously disappointed, but not in the manner that I had feared. After the initial anger, things eventually calmed down, and they started to focus their attention on what I needed to do next. By doing this, I then developed a new plan, which would move me forward and I became far more motivated to make amends.

In the following year, I revisited my exams and achieved better grades and, at the same time, took up my passion for art, which led me to dream of a new career path towards graphic design. It was around this time that I had begun to work part-time in McDonald's at weekends and I discovered that I enjoyed it. I made friends there that are still with me today. It also generated some useful cash, which seemed to keep my Mom happy when I was flunking my studies. I think it helped her maintain her pride in me and the family when there was little else to say positively about me at that time.

Chapter Two – Chasing Status

Whilst earning money was a positive thing for me, I would continually hear stories from my Mom about other kids in our community who were around my age, heading for University studying to do be lawyers, doctors and such like. Every time she went shopping for Indian groceries, she would come back with another update, and inform me of their progress. Whilst she never actually spoke aloud, I could sense that she was disappointed in my choice of education and that she was somewhat frustrated. She felt that I was destined for greater things, and more so, just as capable to succeed in the kind of status that the other kids were endeavouring to achieve.

The Indian community was very close-knit back then and formed a key part of my life, as it does to this day. Education was an important part of our lives, and as such, its significance was overwhelming in terms of perceived status. All the family members would gather to celebrate festivals such as Diwali and important historical dates such as Indian Independence Day. Over the years I was 'actively encouraged' to attend Gujarati School (our native language) and take part in our sports club. Nevertheless, just like in school I found it difficult to fit in at times, not because I did not belong there, but because many of the big personalities (especially in the sports club), were from wealthy families. It is not that we were poor by any stretch of the imagination, but I felt I was always on the outside trying to be accepted into the group, and therefore at times I guess I felt inferior and needed to prove myself worthy.

The college option was not working out for me the way that I had hoped. I was caught in the romance of creating graphics, posters and clever slogans, but the course I was doing kept presenting the opportunity to draw old naked men and women – it was not what I had signed up for.

Working at McDonald's was a great experience for me. I was able to be the real 'me' and I felt at home with the people there; but at the end of the day, it was flipping burgers and that was not going to be a long-term career option.

I have been fortunate in my life that I have always had people look out for me. I had an auntie called Priti, who worked in a bank and she happened to mention to my Mom that there were some opportunities for part-time work – I decided to give it a shot.

The interview was stressful – I mean this was a bank – was I going to be good enough to get this? Thankfully, I got through and began my career at HFC Bank, processing applications for interest free credit for stores like 'Colorvision' and 'World of Leather'. Very quickly, I got into the flow. The job involved talking to sales staff, who you would end up speaking to several times during the course of each day. I began to build some great relationships and really began to enjoy the work, while picking up the odd extra shift when I could.

Eventually, I became so disenfranchised with college that I decided to quit, which allowed me the opportunity to work at the bank on a full-time basis. They were just about to launch the GM Card and, as a result, had some exciting opportunities. It appeared that I had a natural ability to communicate well with people; I was good on the phone, got things done and, in a short period of time, I was promoted, which delighted my Mom. Soon, I was supervising a small team and she enjoyed telling friends and relatives that I was a Bank Manager. Of course, that was not strictly true, but I did not attempt to interfere with her happiness and being able to share with the community that her son was making progress in the world.

It was at this time in my life that I began to feel more confident about myself, a real sense of self-belief, which was to guide me to one of the most important themes of my timeline. Despite that fact that I did not have an auspicious start to my working life in a culture that expected you to work hard and succeed, it was through a mixture of hard work and being in the right place and the right time that I had showed the signs of a corporate career.

I spent four years at HFC, and in that time, I learned a number of lessons. I found that relationships were 'king' – this is something that would prove to be invaluable later in life. I found that if you took genuine joy in serving people and helping them to get what they want, in the long run, this would be returned to you tenfold. My primary motive was not the return on my own investment but the genuine desire to help people – that would be my greatest asset!

As my experience developed further, I would talk to people in other departments. I was always curious about how other areas performed in their duties and acknowledged that what I did would have an impact on them. Throughout my journey of curiosity and, along with my helpful nature, I found that whenever opportunities arose I always seemed to be in consideration for that position. I went from taking applications on the phone, to leading a project with a new client, to working in underwriting, approving loans and ended my stint in the fraud department.

As is with my nature I get bored very quickly. I need to change to keep me interested, so as my career at HFC seemed to be stagnating a little, I then began to look elsewhere for more exciting opportunities. Again, my auntie made a significant intervention. She had heard about a new bank launching in the UK and that I should apply for some of the openings that they had advertised. So I did. I applied for the roll of mortgage underwriter – although I had underwritten loans, the mortgage business was entirely different – the sums of money involved far outweighed anything that I had previously encountered. As I filled out the application form, doubts began to enter my mind. I did not hold much hope of getting an interview (as my experience was lacking) and so I was a little blasé in completing the form – but you know what – that was the real me. Besides, they needed ten years of references so there was not point trying to be 'creative'!

I sent off the application and heard nothing back for a while until one day I received a letter inviting me to an interview. It was with the HR manager. To say I was terrified would be an understatement!

Having pulled myself together, I went along to the interview. As I entered the company's recruitment office, a very enthusiastic and friendly young lady greeted me. She put me at ease in no time at all, and feeling relaxed, I took a seat. After what appeared to be an eternity (but in reality was probably only a matter of minutes) I was summoned to a room where I was greeted by the HR manager. We started chatting and after an hour and a half later, I finally emerged from the interview room. Walking back to my car, I could not make up my mind on how the interview had gone. She had asked me many questions about my attitude towards the job; how I felt about customer service, etc., but I could not recall one single question in terms of underwriting. How odd I thought?

I had not heard anything for a few weeks and by that time, life at HFC was becoming increasingly tedious. Opportunities were drying up and I had had enough of calling people up to inform them that their credit cards had been stolen. Then – out of the blue – I got the call. I got the job. I was ecstatic! The money was substantially more than I was on at the time and I felt like a million dollars.

The job was for Prudential. They had seen an opportunity in the market to establish their own bank and as it was a new bank rather than an offshoot, this meant that they had to apply for a banking license. If the license were granted, it would mean that Prudential Banking was the first new bank for 100 years in the UK.

Being a new bank, everything was new. We were in a new building, which was not completely finished. There were only a handful of people already employed – in fact; I think I was in the third tranche of employees into the company.

It was July 1996 and I arrived on site for day one of training, which was scheduled to last for six weeks. That seemed a lot; up until then my experience of training was a day or half a day in a training room, or one-to-one tuition with a more experienced person. The other thing I noticed was that most of the other people in my group had no prior or very little banking experience, which again I thought was odd, considering this was supposed to be a new bank.

As the training began, it was very clear that this was going to a very different place to work. Different in a good way! We spent a lot of time talking about company culture, organizational values, and vision for the first week, followed by a real focus on what made great customer service and how to communicate effectively. At various points in the training we would be visited by senior Prudential Assurance Management, including the then CEO Jim Sutcliffe. He seemed a really nice man – very down to earth and personable – not at all how I imagined a CEO to be. The same could be said of Mike Harris, who was CEO of the bank.

Prudential were still in the process of being approved for their license and so we were often visited by the Bank of England. This is where I believe my love of public speaking was born. You see, as part of the evidence to show the training was working we were asked to present back to the senior figures at the Bank of England what we had learned. The trainer split us up into groups and we were given a brief. I do not remember much about the specific presentation but all I know was that I was the elected speaker for our group. I was nervous. My palms were sweating and my stomach was in knots as we waited our turn. Then suddenly – we were up. I got on my feet and I do not know what happened next; however, the only way that I can describe it is that I was possessed by something, because my mouth opened and I was in flow. I did not know where the information was coming from but the reaction from the audience was good nevertheless.

I got great feedback from the trainer and from that moment onwards, any opportunity I was presented with to speak in front of people, I grasped with both hands.

Prudential Banking had a very different culture to HFC; that is not to say that HFC was a bad place to work, there was just a fundamental difference in how things were done at Prudential Banking. To begin with, the office was open plan and everyone from CEO to customer service adviser sat out on the floor. As well as a clear vision statement, there were a clear set of shared company values such as, "make a difference in everything we do" and "get it done together and have fun". Now, many companies have a vision statement and/or company values; the difference at Prudential Banking was that theirs did not live on a plaque in the lobby. The vision and values were central to everything that Prudential Banking did, being they were first and foremost.

This is not a business book but it is important for you to understand the culture there, which proved to be a vital ingredient in following the steps towards my career.

Being in that 'start up' environment was exciting. As there were only a few of us we got to know each other well, which was a good thing because after the Bank of England granted Prudential an official banking license, things just went a little crazy. At the time we were only offering mortgages and savings accounts, but we had market beating terms and rates, which resulted in an influx of applications that we had not quite expected.

Soon after, things began to settle down and the signs were that everything was going well. I continued to work in the underwriting team for a few months and then the boredom set in once again. I had enjoyed working in the team but the work was becoming monotonous, so I started to look around for new and more enlightening opportunities. I got chatting to a few people about what else I could do – unbeknown to me at the time – this was my early attempt at networking!

I looked at the team leader and managers that we had and felt like they were the group to be a part of. I saw them as smart, successful people and felt that I could make a valuable contribution to the team, which would mean more money, too.

I approached the head of the department in which I worked and had a long chat about my desire to want to do more. He listened intently and then told me about an upcoming project, which he thought I might be interested in. I would be working alongside a couple of senior managers to set an internal mortgage brokerage service. You see, as a new bank, Prudential had tight criteria and some mortgages just didn't fit; so rather than turn the business away, the idea was to partner with other specialist mortgage providers who could provide products that would match the clients' needs such as 100% or buy to let products.

It was to be set up from scratch. That involved selecting the lenders, setting up the team and designing the processes – all of which would give the perfect opportunity to impress and make my mark.

The project went well. The opportunity to meet prospective partners and even set up meetings to have them come and meet me was an overwhelming experience. This was quite a massage for my ego; my phone would ring and reception would announce that there was a visitor to see me. I worked closely with the HR team to run adverts for more staff, conducted interviews and made decisions on whom to hire. I was also asked to run a number of road shows to the direct sales force to sell the idea of the brokering service. It was a lot fun and I got to work with some great people.

Life was good. Finally, I was feeling like I was making good progress. A key moment I remember was having business cards printed. It seems silly now, but opening that box and seeing my name in print with the title 'manager' underneath was a special moment for me.

I was soon earning more money and bought my first home at twenty-two and a nearly new car. I loved telling people that I was a homeowner... especially to the guys whom I hung out with at the temple, it made me feel that we were now on a more equitable level with one another. My family seemed happier, too. I could see the pride in their eyes. The more successful I became – the more I seemed to be loved – and the more I was accepted.

In 1998, the team at Prudential Banking was hatching a new plan. They had developed a new idea, and one that would transform the financial services market in the UK. This was the birth of *egg.com*.

I had moved on from the Mortgage Brokerage project, taking on a role in the marketing and product development team. I had never had any previous experience of that kind of thing, but the new manager had several chats with me and I suppose he saw something in me that created the opportunity for me to join his team. I could not believe it – me! – In marketing? I had to pinch myself.

I was now mixing with the big boys. I was working closely with consultants and contractors who were drafted in to help the launch of *egg*. These were smart, successful people and it was like being in a different world. I heard many rumours about what kind of daily rate some of these people were on and it was jaw dropping. They talked about different things; they read books and sometimes it felt like they were talking in a different language, too. They had nice cars, houses and a rock star lifestyle...the perfect life...or so it seemed to a twenty-three-year old. That old feeling on inferiority started to creep back in. I was not earning as much, my car was a clapped out Nissan Micra, and I shopped at Top Man!

Looking back at that time, I can see that a shift had occurred in me. I had created the association that success was all about what you have – the big house, the car, and the title. I had also created the belief that if I were 'successful', then ultimately, I would be loved and respected by more people. It was not all negative...I began to read books again and learn some interesting stuff, which would come in very useful later in life.

Egg's culture would be similar to that of Prudential Banking. There was a clear vision and a set of values, which everyone was bought into. In addition, they sent all employees at all levels on a five-day residential programme called 'Touch'. By the time I was due to go on the programme, the stories were already doing the rounds of people coming back from the course and making big changes in their lives, such as breaking up with long-term partners, crying and revealing their deep secrets and all sorts. I have to say, as open as I was to new learning – I was apprehensive about the whole experience.

The day arrived. I made the journey to the hotel and met up with the rest of the group. I think there were about thirty of us and like the courses before we were a mix of different departments, levels and locations. It was nice to meet more people and make more friends.

The course was amazing. It was my first real exposure to personal development. We talked about mindset, positive attitudes, self-belief and self-esteem, as well as the business stuff of customer experience. I did not appreciate it at the time but what I learnt on those five days would provide me with the tools I would need to deal with the biggest moment in my life, which would become the catalyst for my journey.

Chapter Three – Failing in love

Growing up as a teenager, I was never a hit with the ladies – in actual fact – I made David Brent look like Casanova. I never really had a girlfriend, except for a girl in my nursery school who would hold my hand when we watched Play School, but that was about it. I was the archetypal nice guy, whereas any girl that I ever had a crush on would immediately want to be "just good friends". I think it was partly down to a lack of confidence and partly the cultural conflict; you see it was still frowned upon to be dating girls without any prospect of marriage, which therefore made having a steady girlfriend all the more demanding.

It was not such a big deal in my early teens, as most of my time was spent playing cricket or hanging out with my friends; but as I left school and moved into the world of college, it all started to show up. Having screwed up at school, I had to make different choices about what I would study, as my friends had all passed with flying colours. A by-product of that was by way of making new friends – new friends with new interests – girls.

In all other aspects of my life, I was a pretty confident, but when it came to the opposite sex, I just could not pull myself together. In fact, for someone who loved to speak in public I was somewhat silent in those situations!

However, thankfully for me things would change. I had been taking an active part in my community through performing traditional Indian dancing. My parents were enthusiasts and managed to convince me, some of my friends, and other kids in our community to try it. It was a lot of fun and we created a real tight bond as a group. We entered national competitions, performed in front of the Lord Mayor of Birmingham and many other events across the country. In 1997, I started to have more of an interest in Bollywood dancing, and as much of the original group had gone off to uni, been married or lost interest, I started to help my Mom teach the next group.

In preparing for these shows, we would hold practice sessions at my house. Normally parents would drop off and pick up the girls but sometimes we would want to practice longer so I volunteered to drop the girls off at home each night. On the journey back we would chat and discuss ideas about routines and changes, etc.; it was a good little group. Over time, I found that I felt most comfortable to one of the girls in particular.

Now, as this is my story told from my perspective, I want to be respectful and therefore I have used made up names in this chapter.

Her name was Shanti, she was normally my last drop off, and we would end up chatting for ten minutes or so before she got out of the car. I do not quite know what it was, but I was completely comfortable in her presence. It was the real me – no bravado, no front – just me.

There was a bit of an age gap between us; she was just seventeen and I was twenty-one but we did get on really well. I started to develop stronger feelings for her and the drop offs would become the highlight of my week. I remember an occasion when I had taken the scenic route so we could spend longer talking to one another. I was in a confused state. Although I liked her, I was not sure whether she felt the same way about me and the age gap also played on my mind. Eventually I approached my folks for some advice. I think the fact Shanti and her family was known to us, played a significant role – as they told me to go for it.

It was Shanti's birthday, so I thought what better time to declare my feelings. On the drive to her house, the niggling doubt kept coming into my mind telling me that she would not be interested and that I should turn around and save face. Nevertheless, I ignored all the self-talk and arrived at her house. I sat in the car – my heart was pounding, and sweat surfacing on my palms – if I was holding a Martini it would have been shaken not stirred for sure!

I approached the front door and pressed the doorbell – well eventually – as my finger hovered over it for what seemed to be an eternity. After a few nervous seconds, the door opened and there she was with a somewhat surprised look on her face. "Oh, happy birthday!" I said in a slightly higher pitched voice under the strain from nerves. Shanti invited me in and after an uncomfortable silence lasting several minutes (actually it was a few seconds but it felt so much longer than that) I told her how I felt. I was bracing myself for the rejection speech that I had heard so often; but, to my surprise, Shanti felt the same way and was somewhat relieved that I had made the first move as she herself thought I never would, and how right she nearly was! I left her house and went home with a smile on my face. I felt like a giant inside.

Today things are a little different but within the Indian community, dating without marriage back then was considered to be a "no go area". We both had to tell our folks and both sets of parents were happy, though her parents were concerned about the age gap and did not want any talk of marriage too soon...but the expectation that it would happen was very real indeed.

The relationship blossomed, and being together seemed like the most natural thing in the world. A year in and we were swept along by the very nature of our culture; our engagement was arranged. The engagement party is an important and essential part of an Indian culture – it is the formal approval of the relationship by the extended families. Our parents were proud and looking forward to the day that their eldest son would be married.

We had over 400 guests including my family from India. I was so overwhelmed by the occasion that the day was a bit of blur to be honest, but enjoyable in the sense that I had my whole family and loved ones around.

After the engagement, the next the phase was to plan the wedding and chief wedding planning duty went to the parents. It was still at least a year away but there was a much to be done...shopping trips to India, invitations, organizing catering, etc.

Shortly after the engagement, I moved house and into a bigger accommodation. Work was getting busy after the launch of *egg*. I guess you could say it was pretty normal. Although we were spending time together, it was at lots of family functions as people were keen for her to integrate into the family. The time we did spend alone was clouded by a feeling of distance...I did get the sense that things were not all rosy in the garden, but I just figured it was stress and pre-wedding nerves.

As the wedding machine was in full swing, I started to get more and more evidence that something was seriously wrong. I thought about whether I should call things off, but the family was happy and everyone in the community knew about us, what would it do to our families' reputation?

Just a few weeks before the wedding, Shanti pulled out of the relationship. I got a phone call at work from her Dad asking me to pop over and see him. I thought nothing of it, as it was fairly routine and figured he might want to talk about the wedding arrangements. What was odd was that he called back a short time later and insisted I brought my parents along.

We arrived at the house none the wiser about what was about to happen. From the moment I knocked on the door I got this unnerving feeling that something bad was about to happen. We entered the house and as we turned left into the living room from the hallway, the situation became clear. They had invited a mutual friend of the family along. There was no eye contact from anybody and then her Dad calmly said that "the wedding should be called off". It turned out that she did not love me any longer; my heart sank and I looked at the expression on my parent's faces. I controlled my initial anger, and then calmly stood up and walked out of the house. Her parents tried to stop me but I marched out of the front door and kept going, and it was at that point that something strange occurred to me. As the cold spring air hit my face, the feeling of being broken-hearted began to subside to be replaced by what I can only describe as a sense of relief. I felt like this huge weight had been lifted from my shoulders. Being the eldest son; the eldest grandson, and the first to be married in the family, the pressure that was on my shoulders was intense, therefore I had ignored my own intuition, just to appease my family and follow the path that was expected of me.

I walked around the block, and my mind began to wonder. At first, I was concerned with what people would say and I began to imagine the conversations I would end up having trying to explain what had happened. I began to imagine the embarrassment and shame of it all.

As I made my way round the corner leading back to Shanti's house, I stopped and gave myself a talking to — a kind of pep talk. I told myself that it did not really matter what people said or thought; what mattered most was what I thought. I recalled some of the lessons I had learned about attitude on the 'Touch' course at work and reminded myself that events are just events and it is the meaning we give them that drives our emotions. I could have chosen to give this situation the meaning of shame and embarrassment or I could have taken a different view and seen it as a second chance or opportunity to find my soul mate. I reminded myself that I was the controller of my own destiny.

Once I decided to take a more positive view, I found myself letting go of the anger and instead just accepting that life just had a different plan for me. Naturally, I was disappointed and hurt by the whole thing, but then again, it could have been far worse; what if this had happened closer to the wedding? What if it had happened after we were married? What if she had not been brave enough to call it off?

I found myself back at Shanti's front door. I composed myself with a cloud of deep breaths and rang the bell. I walked in and told my parents that we should leave; there was nothing left to discuss or to be gained from trying to figure out what was going on. If Shanti truly did not love me anymore, then this was the best solution all round – and with nothing further to discuss – we left.

The drive home was almost in silence. I just sat and stared out of the window at the stars and quietly assured myself that something special was ahead...and boy was that an understatement...

Chapter Four – Meeting Jem

Like most things in my life, meeting Jem was anything but straightforward, and yet it was certainly where fate and destiny began to create havoc in my life.

Almost immediately after Shanti called off the wedding, the phone began to ring with well-intentioned family members who were attempting to resell me into other families. It was great for my ego, furthermore, many had believed that the match was wrong and were keen to tell me about daughters, nieces and sisters that would be a far better match for me. That annoyed me somewhat. If people who were close to me thought that, then why did no one say something to me?

I had no intention of meeting any other girls or considering marriage at that time. In fact, I announced to the Universe that I had had enough of women and, in a clear effort to clear my head and move on with my life, I planned a trip to New York where I would let my hair down and simply enjoy myself.

Days before the trip, my Dad's uncle called at the house with news of a potential partner. He had done the research…families histories matched, the values seemed a good fit, and above all, our initials were the same as my great uncle and his wife, so it just had to be a good match!

My parents approached me with the idea, which I refused point blank. How could I?! Wasn't it a little early to be thinking about another girl?!

Having slept on it, I woke the next morning and agreed to meet her. I do not know why, but there was something that was telling me that I should. Even then, I would change my mind several times over during the following days, which drove my Dad insane. Finally, some words of wisdom from a close friend, Dipak, settled me down. He said, "What have you got to lose? What if she is the one?"

This was not a true arranged marriage, but more of a facilitated introduction and, as this was the more traditional route, the process involved an initial interview. In essence, it is where the two families would meet, and the boy and girl would chat. I had, however, several details about the girl beforehand, but that was about it. She was a beautician and her name was Jaymini or Jem for short. This was the first time for me, but it turned out that Jem was somewhat an expert on this process. She had already met fourteen guys before me and none had proved to be a suitable match for one reason or another.

Jem and her family lived in Leicester in the East Midlands. Her parents were similar to mine in that her mother (like my Dad), was an immigrant from East Africa whilst her father (like my Mom), came to the UK from India after marriage. They had also had a family business – a general store in Rainhill, which is near Liverpool. It turned out that they had only moved back to Leicester a few years earlier. Jem's father had suffered from ill health, and a bad fall had confined him to a wheelchair, so they lived in a bungalow on an estate where houses were designed for elderly or disabled people. Normally they would arrange interviews to take place at Jem's brother's place, as it was bigger and created a better first impression.

However, Jem was fed up with all these meetings and she really was no longer interested in further interviews. When she was told about me, she told her parents that I would just have to come and see her at their home, as she did not want the rigmarole of setting things up at her brother's home – take it or leave it was her ultimatum to her Mom. In similar fashion, I decided on the 'come as you are' approach. Normally in these meetings, the boys would dress up a little – you know – all suited and booted. Not me, I decided to go as the real me and, if she was really was the one for me, then it would not bother her.

We took the short journey up the M69 to Leicester, and as we got closer, I started to wonder about the guys that had been to see Jem before me. What was it about them she did not like? Would I be any different? I started to wonder if this girl really could be the one.

We pulled up outside the house, I did not notice at the time; however, Jem's brother snuck a peak through the curtains. Apparently, I have a likeness to a Bollywood actor called Akshay Kumar and Jem's brother took delight in passing that message on to her, along with the news that I was different from the others who had come before me.

As I got out of the car and headed up towards the house, I had that feeling once again that someone was trying to tell me something…it was a voice of approval telling me that I was about to take an important step forward in the timeline of Vinay Parmar!

I rang the bell and eagerly awaited an answer, my heart was pounding faster, and the butterflies in my stomach were flying at full speed and my head full of questions and self-talk. When the door opened, my parents and I were greeted by the warmest of smiles and, as I crossed the threshold, I had that warm feeling you get when you arrive home from a long trip…it felt so comfortable.

In the living room were Jem's parents, her brother Reekesh along with her eldest brother Atul and his wife Sheema. Jem was hidden away! The conversation began tentatively, with some small talk, but was soon in full flow as we chatted about our families and identified common connections. I soon forgot why I was there until my Mom asked when we would meet Jem. Jem was waiting in another room in the house. Her Mom took me through and, as I nervously entered, I was greeted by a very pretty girl. She was stunning! I was truly punching above my weight!

We began chatting – to be more precise – I started talking and talking! I asked her all sorts of questions, while receiving only one-word answers. I got the impression that my conversational wizardry was being wasted and this girl was not going to open up to me – but I knew I liked her!

When we eventually said our goodbyes and got back into the car to head home, my Dad asked me what I thought. As much as I tried to play it cool and hide my feelings, a grin appeared on my face and I said, "She's nice! I'd like to see her again."

By the time we had returned home, Jem's family had informed my Dad that they were interested, too, but understandably were concerned that I had just come out of a relationship, so therefore would prefer to do some independent research on me at first.

I had a busy few days ahead, one of my closest friends, Dipak, was getting married that weekend and I was due to fly out to New York with my other close friend Nilesh on the Monday.

During the pre wedding rituals at Dipak's, all I could do was talk about Jem. I had even managed to get her Mom to give me a photograph of her, which I showed to a select few. How could it be that after just one meeting, Jem was already feeling like an integral part of my life? It was a sign of things to come.

Dipak's wedding went well. Our close group of friends was together again to share in his special day. As I sat and watched the ceremony, I could see the happiness in both bride and groom. I thought quietly to myself, "This could be me soon."

I arrived at Heathrow Airport full of excitement about the trip to the Big Apple, and as I sat in the airport lounge waiting to board my flight, I could not get Jem out of my mind. The uncertainty of not knowing what she was thinking was killing me. I wanted to know but I would have to learn and understand the lesson about the value of patience.

The trip was enjoyable but I was in a completely different mindset to what I had anticipated. I would call home to check if my Mom had heard anything. Each time I heard no, then more doubt would enter my mind and then the more I would convince myself that Jem would never be interested in me.

When I returned back to the UK, I rang my Mom to let her know that I was on my way home, and she told me that she had some good news. She had heard from Jem's family and she wanted to meet up with me again. The plan was for me to go directly to Leicester, as Jem was due to go to India for a holiday within the next few days. The smile on my face was overwhelming! Pedal to the metal and I was in Leicester in no time. This time round Jem was more open, in fact, she interrogated me quite well. We talked for hours and it was then that I knew that I wanted to spend the rest of my life with her.

Soon afterwards, our families agreed a 'Naki', which is a formal agreement between two families that a relationship has begun and a marriage is in the making. Jem and I continued to get to know each other and got invites to each other's family functions, my Mom would make no apologies for showing Jem off at our relatives! It was great to see her with such a proud look on her face. Slowly but surely, Jem and I fell in love...

Chapter Five – Wedding Day

Our engagement ceremony and civil wedding was organized for March 25th 2000. It was a small affair…well, small by Indian standards. We had around a hundred of our closest friends and family enjoy the day with us. Jem looked stunning as always and I had not scrubbed up so badly myself. It was a beautiful spring day; the gaps in the clouds were filled with sunshine, which beamed down on us with a warming glow. It perfectly represented what we had been through over the last eighteen months.

Soon afterwards, the plans for the 'real' wedding were very much in full swing. My parents flew out to India to shop for outfits, gifts, etc. It was like a mini trade expedition! As fate would have it, Jem's Mom would go with them, which meant that they would spend some quality time together. As July 9th approached, there was a feeling of happiness and contentment at home. My Mom was glowing with excitement and the relationship between my Mom and Jem was blossoming. My Mom loved to organize, and organize she did.

Both Jem and I had large families. Over 1000 guests would attend the wedding. Our tradition and culture ensures that the family is extended by way of those families who had previously invited us to their weddings. We had also added many friends that we had made, while also those who were our parents' business associates. It was quite a task to manage a guest list; it could easily have been 2000!

As the day grew closer, my excitement started to grow. For the first time in my life, everything appeared to be falling into place. I was about to be married to an amazing woman who I was deeply in love with. We were preparing for one of the highlights of an Indian family's calendar – the wedding of their first-born son. I had already bought a house and was looking forward to starting our life together with the incredible family that we were fortunate enough to be in.

Brothers, sisters, cousins, nieces, nephews, grandparents, aunties and uncles, were all involved in the preparations for our big day. The venue was booked in Leicester and we prepared my parent's house back in Hall Green – about forty miles away. Our house was transformed with decorations; we even had a marquee on the back as overflow space for the families and friends that would descend upon us for our special day. (I am not sure how much you will know about an Indian wedding, but they are certainly not one-day affairs!) Our weddings last several days, beginning with ceremonies taking place at both bride and bridegrooms' home. The first of the ceremonies is to invoke the gods, bring blessings and remove all the bad spirits.

The second most important thing in Indian culture aside from weddings is food. The house was filled with the aroma of beautifully cooked vegetarian food as well as being fully stocked with Indian sweets. As I sat back, I watched the team of relatives and friends my Mom had assembled to help, and I could see her beaming from ear to ear. I could see the sense of pride and excitement oozing through her.

The last of the rituals was being held off site. Everyone had left, except for a couple of friends. I was not allowed to leave the house, as it was considered to be bad luck. Therefore, I sat quietly and contemplated what was about to happen. I thought to myself, *This time tomorrow I will be a married man*. I could not wait!

My Mom arrived back at the house earlier than expected, saying that she felt tired. She was a bit under the weather and wanted an early night. She had worked really hard so it was not really too much of a surprise. I took her up a couple of paracetamol and a hot water bottle. Jem and her Mom called the house, and the two of them shared a joke about turning up on time. Mom had a quick chat with Jem and then went to sleep.

As I lay in my bed sleeping, something entered our house. It was not a person, an animal or even a ghost – it was destiny! – and it was about to make another decisive move...

I woke that day with a spring in my step. I leapt out of my makeshift bed and headed for the shower. As I got to the top of the stairs, I could hear a commotion coming from my parent's bedroom. The door was ajar, so I entered slowly. I could not believe what I was seeing. There, lying on the bed, almost lifeless and with a rash covering her body was my Mom. She could not speak much and was unable to focus her vision to make me out, even though I was standing right in front of her.

I experienced a sinking feeling in my heart. I knew that something was seriously wrong. Ricky, my youngest brother, was at University and recently there had been a student who had died from a disease called meningitis. There had been a lot of information posted around and the symptoms my Mom had, appeared to match them.

I did what they call a tumbler test, where you take a glass and roll it against the skin to see if the rash subsides – it did not – "Quick! Call 999!" I shouted. As we waited for the ambulance, I could see that she was getting worse. We had organized coaches to take family and friends to Leicester and as they arrived, so did the paramedics. It was a harrowing vision – one I thought I would never witness.

The paramedics checked Mom over but they were unable to determine the cause of her illness. "It could be chicken pox or measles," said one of the paramedics.

I thought to myself, *Well, that's OK! She will get better.*

After further questions and tests, the paramedics decided to take her to the emergency room. "We will take her in for some tests," said the lead paramedic.

"She's going to be OK, right?" I asked.

"You should go ahead. She will probably join you after the tests," said the other paramedic.

Dad tried to assure me that everything would be OK and that I should carry on with all the rituals, preparations and ceremonies for the day. The family had been preparing for this for days and things had to continue. As the ambulance crew led my Mom down the stairs, she turned to look at me and it was then when I looked into her eyes I could see that she was in pain. The house was full of family and they were all stunned as to what was happening. I could hear the whispers begin…

I turned around and headed back downstairs to complete the ceremonies. I sat in a chair and put on a brave front as my aunties continued with the rituals and blessings; yet, all the while my mind was elsewhere. How was I going to get through this?

As I made my way out of the house and into the wedding car, I could see the expressions of angst on the faces of the guests. Most people had made the assumption something had happened to my grandma, but were shocked when my Mom emerged with the paramedics. Minutes later, the ambulance carrying my Mom, headed off to the right – my wedding car – headed left in the other direction. This was to be a significant move, as life was about to take my Mom and I in different directions.

The journey to Leicester was somewhat of a blur. I tried to call my Dad but there was no answer…I grew more and more anxious.

Just as we arrived in Leicester, a message came through to say that my Mom was waiting to be seen by the doctors, leaving me with a sense of encouragement. *She is in the right place and the doctors will take care of her, right?* I asked myself.

I began to feel more positive. A real smile appeared on my face for probably the first time that day. We finally approached the venue for the wedding, which was being held in a school hall (where else could you house a 1000 guests?!). As we drove up the driveway, Jem's (extended) family was waiting outside to welcome me. The news had not reached all of them, although Jem's parents and close family knew that my Mom was ill, albeit neither of us was aware to what extent.

I got out of the car and met my mother-in-law, who greeted me and took me inside. It was like walking through a rainbow with so many beautiful colours that were being worn by so many beautifully dressed ladies. Traditional wedding songs were being sung – I would like to say that they sounded harmonic – but clearly some singing lessons were required by some.

Without my parents present, somebody else in the family would have to perform their duties in the ceremony. A debate then erupted! I wanted my youngest uncle and aunt to do it, as I had always been very close to them, although other people had different ideas. Tradition and culture meant that my Dad's eldest brother was to be given the privilege; however, we had not spoken for almost fifteen years, after he and my Dad had fallen out over business. He was only there because my Mom saw the wedding as an opportunity to forgive and forget, which she hoped would bring the family together. I was angry! I could have made a real scene, but I understood it would upset the occasion further and, more significantly; it would upset Jem's family, so I went along with it.

The ceremony began and I felt myself being drawn into the wonder of the music; the smells, the colours and the atmosphere of the day. It was a traditional set-up with the wedding ceremony taking place front and centre stage. Weirdly, it was like being at the front of the class during assembly at school. The priest was informed of the situation, and as such, we asked him to hurry things up a little.

As is tradition, it is bad luck to see the bride before the wedding, so Jem was well hidden. In Hindu weddings, a drape or curtain is held in front of the groom so he cannot see his bride making an entrance. In traditional style, Jem was led down the aisle by her maternal uncles. She made her way up the steps, carefully, and was seated opposite me. Our hands were placed together from underneath the curtain, which was still in place, while the priest performed another ritual. Eventually, the curtain dropped and there she was, sitting opposite me. She was full of radiance and beauty! Everything seemed to be a parallel world to the chaos and confusion that I had left behind at home.

The ceremony was now in full swing. Every now and then, I would glance over at my family and catch them on mobile phones and in huddled conversation. Each time I asked how my Mom was, I was given reassuring words that there was no change and that they were still doing tests.

About midway through the ceremony, I had the most unusual experience of my life. I suddenly got this feeling that someone had reached inside my chest and pulled something out. It was as if something had left me suddenly and I just broke down in tears of despair. "Something has happened to my Mom! Tell me the truth!" I shouted across to my family. Some of my cousins gathered around me and tried to calm me down. Seeing me in this state had clearly upset Jem, and she was in tears, too. Eventually my cousins managed to calm me down and they reassured me that everything was OK. I took a few deep breaths and drank some water.

Jem and I did our best to enjoy the ceremony, although both of my parents were missing. It was clear to both of us that this was not going to be the day that we had envisioned.

Eventually, the ceremony ended, and we were ushered away by my aunt, as the situation at home had taken a turn for the worse.

Chapter Six – Time To Say Good Bye

Having cut the post-wedding rituals short, we were now heading back down the M69 towards home. The car was silent; I knew that the situation had gotten worse with my Mom; however, I had received no further information at this time. I kept thinking, how bad could it be? Maybe Mom was just having some emergency treatment; but all the while, I just assumed that she would pull through.

We arrived at my home where one of my closest friends Kamal, was waiting for me. He was forever smiling – a real happy-go-lucky type. When I saw the look on his face, I began to get the feeling that things were not good. He rushed Jem and me into his car and sped us over to Heartlands Hospital. We headed towards the intensive care unit and, although still dressed in our wedding attire, we began to run to the ward.

Kamal, Jem and I got in the lift to the upper floors where the family was. As the doors opened, I saw the sign for the High Dependency Unit, and as I turned to my right, there was my Dad, distraught – clearly, he had been crying. Both of my younger brothers were in, too, and they looked like their eyes had taken a beating. My Dad embraced me and broke down: "Your Mom is dying!" he shouted. I could not believe what had he just said.

It took a few minutes to get the full story. My Mom was seriously ill with a lethal strain of meningitis. Her heart had already stopped once, her organs were failing, and she was being kept alive by a life support machine. Due to a lack of room, she had been looked after in the High Dependency Unit but was now being rushed up to the Intensive Care Unit.

We were all taken to a waiting area. Some of my family was already there, and looks of hopelessness decorated their faces. I still had not seen my Mom yet. It was then that I heard a commotion; the nurses were bringing up a patient – it was my Mom – I caught the faintest glimpse of her as they rushed past.

A few minutes later a doctor came in to tell us we could go through and see her. I will never forget the next few moments. They happened in slow motion. Jem and I walked through the double doors and as they swung back, they revealed my Mom lying lifeless with what seemed like a dozen drips attached to her. Her face was swollen; she wore an oxygen mask and there was blood gently dripping from her nose. It seemed as though she was weeping, as what appeared to be tears, fell from her tightly closed eyes. Jem and I stood there and cried. I held my Mom's hand and pleaded with her to respond and give a sign that she was still with us. No sign was of forthcoming.

A short while later the consultant came to see us. He took us into his office. It was a small room with a few books on a shelf and papers piled on the corner of a desk. He sat in his chair behind the desk, as we took seats the other side. He took a deep breath, looked at me and delivered the prognosis. My Mom was not responding to the drugs she was being given; all her major organs had failed, and she was being kept alive by a machine. I could not comprehend what he was saying, just 24hrs earlier she was fine and now...now she was all but dead.

The consultant's next statement was to send my head into spin even further. He talked to us about making a decision on how long we left the life support machine running. I felt a sense of anger come over me – how dare he suggest we switch the machine off! Why were they giving up on her so easily? By this time, I had become the spokesperson for the family and I bluntly refused to consider anything to do with the life support machine. With that, we all left the room and headed back to the ward where my Mom lay at the mercy of this lethal disease.

I would love to tell you that some miracle took place and my Mom came through but sadly, it did not. There was no hope; our decision to keep the life support machine running was one of emotion and not logic. In the final few hours with her at her bedside, I made promises that I would look after the family and that I would take care of my Dad. I wanted her to know that everything would be OK. There was nothing more we could do for her, so we went home for the night. We were naturally clinging to any glimmer of hope, and in the early hours of the morning, the call came through to say that her condition had worsened severely and that we should attend the hospital. We spent a short time talking to the consultant before deciding that enough was enough, and with that came the biggest decision of my life so far – to turn off that life support machine. I could not bear to be with her when they switched it off but once she had passed, I went in to see her for one last time. Her skin was still warm and it appeared that she had been crying. She looked so peaceful, as if she was sleeping and I swear I thought she would get up at any moment.

My Mom was just 49 years old.

We all dealt with the situation in different ways. I just felt empty inside. I was not as tearful as my Dad, my wife, or my brothers...I just do not think it had quite hit me.

Having heard the news, family and friends greeted us when we returned home from the hospital. Everyone sat and prayed, chanting God's name, but that was the last thing I wanted to do. I was angry: *How could God do this to us?* I asked myself. *Why should I now chant the name of God who has caused such pain to my family?*

The rumour mill soon started with stories circulating as to what had happened, how my Mom had died and debates ensued as to why it happened. Some stories suggested that Mom had died before the wedding and we had covered it up so we could continue with the wedding. Other stories claimed that we had made some kind of mistake during the rituals and therefore God had punished us. What really shocked me though was the suggestion that somehow it was Jem's fault, that she had brought bad luck on the family. How could people even think that? I am not for superstition but I know that Jem's family were worried that there may be some repercussions; I think they may have feared that we would buy into that theory. My Dad acted quick to defuse the situation; when Jem's family arrived, he reassured them that we did not believe in that kind of thing and that Jem was a part of our family now.

I did not care for all the stories and instead I began to focus on the practicalities. With the help of a couple of my uncles, I started to call round family and friends to tell them the news. At first, it was difficult, as I would choke up with tears, not just because of my own emotions but also due to reaction on the other end of the phone. The more I did it, the more hardened I think I became; it was almost matter-of-fact.

Next job was to organize the funeral. I was only 25 at the time, and my life experience had not yet provided me with the type of situations where I could have learnt what to do. Thankfully, I had the support of my best friends along with my uncle and brother-in-law. They took care of everything, from organizing the funeral director to collecting the death certificate.

Later in that morning, my Mom's sister arrived from India. She had not been able to make it to the wedding but had managed to get a flight to surprise my Mom the day after. I cannot imagine what she must have gone through on the flight over, knowing that her eldest sister had passed, and having lost her own husband only six months earlier.

The owner of the company whom we hired the marquee from was so saddened by what had happened that he let us keep it up without any additional costs. It came in useful, as over the next few days the house was to be full of family, friends, neighbours and members of our Indian community who would come to pay their respects. I was overwhelmed by it all; I met people I did not even know, yet people who my Mom had helped in some way shape or form. She touched so many people's lives in such a positive way, and in the midst of all the dark feelings, I began to feel a sense of pride.

The day of the funeral was fast approaching and preparations were being made. As practicing Hindus, we would have a cremation. There were rituals and traditions to follow, which were supposed to give my Mom's soul peace in the afterlife. You see, the Hindu religion teaches us that the body is just a vehicle for the eternal soul, which then moves on to take a new form when its current life cycle is over. I found that difficult to grasp. Believing the theory is one thing – but when you actually experience a death of a loved one – it is hard to accept.

Our traditions meant that my Mom's body would be brought home to allow us to complete rituals. It meant having an open casket – my Dad did not want that – none of us did. My Mom's body had disfigured and swelled so much that we did not want the way she looked to be the final memory we held of her. Unfortunately, other people had different ideas. Again, superstitions, traditions and cultural obligations meant that my Dad was pretty much forced into going with an open casket by elders and other senior members of the extended family.

I do not really remember much of the actual day of the funeral except that the hearse carrying her coffin arrived early that morning. There were already people at house ready to pay their respects. I can recall that during the rituals people kept telling us (my Dad especially) repeatedly not to cry as this would bring pain to my Mom's soul. We were mourning a deep, tragic loss; surely, there was room to express the most natural of human emotions?

The rest of the day was a blur, up until the point where we were at the crematorium and pressed the button on the podium, which sent the coffin through to begin the process. I had been at funerals before and seen families do this, as the coffin would disappear behind the long draped curtains, I would often wonder what was behind them and be curious as to where the coffin when next. Well I was about to find out.

Once the coffin was out of sight, we were led to what I can only describe as an observatory, which overlooked the furnace below. Moments later, my Mom's coffin came through...it suddenly struck me how final this was. It may sound strange, but even though she was dead, her body was still with us and that had given me some comfort; however, what was happening now would mean I would never see her again. I remember Ricky, my youngest brother just falling to his knees as he broke down into tears. He pressed himself against the glass yelling down to my Mom in the coffin as it slowly moved into the furnace.

Then it was done. She was gone in every sense of the phrase.

We headed back to house for more rituals. As the eldest son, I would be called upon to perform most of them. It was strange, but the experience at the crematorium somehow brought a sense of calm to my soul, as if it was some kind of closure on the whole event.

Chapter Seven – The Great Depression

In the days that followed the funeral, fewer and fewer people were at the house. My closest friends and key members of my family were normally around, but other people returned to their somewhat normal lives. It would be soon after that those closest to us would also leave – their lives would continue as they had always done so – the turmoil of my life had only just begun.

I would stay awake at night sometimes asking *why me? What had I done to deserve this? Was I not good person?* Other times I felt full of guilt, *was I too hasty with the decision to switch off the machine? What if Mom had pulled through! What if I had killed her!*

Again, I found myself in the all too familiar place of being caught in two worlds. In my culture, being the 'big brother' carries a large responsibility; he is there to take care of his younger siblings and is expected to look after his folks, as they get older. I felt that obligation to take care of things and provide support. I was cautious not to be visibly upset in front of them; my strategy would be to try to divert attention or lighten the mood as much as possible. In the process, I had developed a hard exterior, which the outside world saw as me being 'strong'.

Inside it was a completely different story. At times, I felt like I was being eaten alive. I could not express my true feelings except when I was alone with Jem, and even then, I was careful not to upset her too much. I was just twenty-five; this was not supposed to be happening to me. I was supposed to be starting a new chapter in my life with my new bride; however, instead I was overcome with guilt, and fuelled with anger towards God for taking my Mom away from me.

We all handled the grief of losing my Mom in different ways. My Dad fell into a state of depression; not only had he lost his wife but also he had lost his best friend and the rock that had held them together. Both my younger brothers were coming to terms with the fact that Mom would not be there to share in their future. For Jem, she was trying to settle in amongst this emotional cloud. For her, I imagine it was a difficult position, as she would have been upset at the loss of my Mom, and yet she had only known her for a short period of time. I guess she was more upset for me and in shock at the way her married life had started.

I took up some counseling to see if that would help. Whilst it was good to talk to someone unconnected with my family about how I really felt, I found that it focused too much on the past and trying to find reasons why I felt like I did. Looking back to the past served no positive purpose in my eyes; it was not going to change anything after all. I was more interested in understanding how I should move forward.

Instead, the obligation as 'big brother' did more to focus me on the road ahead; it gave me a greater sense of purpose. I was not doing this just for me or to be some kind of hero; I was doing it for the family. I was doing it for my Mom. I turned my attention to all the practical things that needed to be done, like dealing with probate, insurance companies and banks. It is a surreal experience calling complete strangers and telling them that your mother has died. Everything for me was about the next step – what needed doing next.

My Grandma had been living with us my whole life but at 88, she was now entering the twilight of her life and suffering from the onset of dementia. She was not yet in state where she needed full-time care, but she was approaching that stage. Before my Mom died, she along with my Dad would take care of her needs. She had a very special relationship with my Mom; we could all see the impact that this loss was having on her, too. We had to think about what to do about her care now, as my Dad was not in the right state to look after her. We were fortunate that my Dad's sister was happy to have Grandma live with them, which took a huge burden off our shoulders.

Whilst we would spend the day at my Dad's place, each evening Jem and I would return to our home which was only a few minutes away. However, it no longer felt like a home; it was just a house now. I felt like I needed to be closer to my Dad so I could support him more and my younger siblings. Jem was also finding it tough being alone, and so we decided that we should buy a bigger house so we could all be together and support each other. That is what we did. I know my Mom had always wanted to move to a bigger house, so it felt – in some way – we were fulfilling one of her dreams, too.

It was not too long before we found the perfect place. It had space for all of us including my Grandma. At last, something to look forward to, or so I thought.

In preparing to move, we began to clear out some of my Mom's things. We filled charity bags with her clothes and belongings. It was hard; you do not quite realize it, but certain things become synonymous with a person. There were fond memories attached to certain clothes – like holidays, presents for Mother's Day and other special occasions. They we just pieces of fabric, but letting go was difficult. It was during that clear out that I made a discovery. Tucked behind her clothes were Mother's Day and Birthday Cards she had kept. I never knew she did that. I always assumed that she threw them out. It stopped me in my tracks. I sat and read through the cards and it brought tears to my eyes – what else was there about her that I did not know – that I would never know?

Eventually I went back to work after an extended period of leave. It was strange going back into the office. The last time I walked out through the revolving glass doors, I was leaving with a spring in my step, as my colleagues wished me well for the wedding; however, I was going to walk back through them in completely different circumstances.

Making my way through the doors, I caught a glimpse of the security guard on the front desk who just gave me an almost apologetic smile and nodded in my direction. I think he had heard the news.

I pressed the call button on the lift and prayed that nobody would be in there when it arrived. I was in luck. When the doors opened on floor 3, I walked out and paused to compose myself before beginning my walk to the middle of the office to my desk and my colleagues. All eyes were on me; I was greeted with the same apologetic smiles and warm smiles as the security guard had given me downstairs. I would smile back in a similar way, as a mark of acknowledgment.

After what seemed an eternity I made it to my desk and sat quietly for a few seconds before hitting the 'on' button my PC. As it booted up with the customary Microsoft Windows chimes, I noticed my colleague Kim sat opposite me. He was from the old school and never really showed much emotion, but looking at his face I could see even he was moved. He asked if I was OK. I answered "yes" – I mean – what else could I say? It was not his fault of course; he was just being polite.

I found that a lot; people were just being polite, not really know-ing what to say to me. Some would even avoid me, as they felt awkward. There would be some polite small talk from them, something like a cliché – "Time is a great healer!" – again, it was no fault of theirs, as none of us are prepared or taught how to approach death with others.

As I began to become more aware of it, I started to change my approach in how to relieve the other person of worrying about what to say. Therefore, I would start with a different conversation or by making some kind of joke in order to make them feel more comfortable.

Each time I would venture out into our community or anytime I ran into someone, I knew that they would always ask about my Dad, my broth-ers and my wife. "Oh, how is your Dad? Make sure you look after him," they would say or, "How is Jaymini coping?" No one ever asked how I was. *Was I not going through this as well? Do I not matter?*

There were certain quarters, mostly men, who were beginning to wonder if my Dad would marry again. It is a cultural thing, where stereotypical men cannot look after themselves. There were even conversations taking place about matching up my Dad to one of my Mom's sisters – it was unreal. I guess some of those people had the right intent at heart but it was never going to be a viable option.

As the 6th month mark approached, we seemed to be settling down a little more. The house move was imminent and my middle brother Dipit, Dad and I, all returned to work, which kept us busy and got us back into a routine. Jem found a job, which got her out and about and Ricky went back to University in Leicester. Some kind of normality had now found the Parmar household.

Festivals, special occasions and key dates are always difficult the first time around when you have lost someone so close to you. Normally, my Mom would make a big deal during festivals like Diwali and Christmas. The house would always be buzzing with excitement; we would be together as a family and my Mom would always have some kind of feast prepared for us to dig into. This year, although we were together for Christmas, it felt like the main ingredient was missing.

I was DJ'ing part time back then, and I had taken a booking for New Year's Eve. I figured I would not be in the mood to party myself but at the same time, I did not want to be moping around at home. A couple of days before the gig, I was preparing my playlist and checking over my equipment when the phone rang. It was my aunt; she was clearly in a traumatic state as my Grandma was feeling unwell, and she asked for my Dad. We immediately headed over to her house, which was just a short drive away. By the time we arrived, my Grandma had calmed down but she still was not herself so we called 999 to be on the safe side. The paramedics came and completed some tests including and ECG, which revealed that she had some kind of heart trauma. She was admitted to hospital where it was later confirmed that she had had a heart attack.

I could not face losing some else I loved so much, so soon after my Mom. My Grandma had been a constant figure in my life. She had lived with us since I was born and we were all close to her, especially my brother Dipit. Thankfully, she was responding to the treatment and was recovering well. I went to visit her everyday but on New Year's Eve, I decided not to as I had a bit of cold and also I wanted to prepare for my gig later that night.

The party was in full flow when suddenly my phone started vibrating in my pocket. It was Jem. She was upset and told me that my Grandma had taken a turn for the worse. She told me I needed to get there as soon as I could. Luckily, I was able to leave the set in the hands of my cousin as I hot- footed it to the hospital. It was too late – by the time I had arrived – she was gone.

It was a different feeling this time. I was upset that she had died but at the same time, with her dementia worsening, it was probably a blessing to some degree.

I had to head back to the party to finish off the job I had been hired to do. Believing that the Universe had conspired against me, I began the New Year countdown: "10, 9, 8, 7, 6, 5, 4, 3, 2, 1" – "Happy New Year!" I shouted over the microphone. Nobody at that party had a clue as to what really went on that night.

I was glad to see the back of the year 2000. I recalled the entire foray about the Millennium bug the year before, and whilst the end of the world never came as some had predicted, it felt like my family had suffered our own Millennium meltdown.

Chapter Eight – All change here

There were to be big changes for the year ahead; we had already moved home, and were now living in Solihull. It was nice to be in a new and fresh environment, one that would conceal the memories of sadness, while attempting to move forward with our lives. Of course, neither my Mom or Grandma would be here to share in the moment; my Mom would have loved our new home, a feeling of contentment that it held when I first came to see it.

The theme of change continued and I felt in order to move on with things, I needed a new challenge and therefore I took up an opportunity to work at large insurance company. They were looking to build something new and I thought it was the perfect project for me to get my teeth into, and besides, it was more money and closer to home (I was travelling over 30 minutes per day each way in my current job), so I could be around more to support my family.

I started with a real sense of purpose and ploughed all my energy into the task ahead. However, this was to prove short-lived, as within six months of me being with the company, the financial services' industry was changing with the many other sales forces that were being cut. This proved to have severe repercussions on how business would move forward; everyone handled the change differently – some were devastated and angry – others merely saw the job as a stopgap for them, so were not overly concerned. For me – I saw things a little differently.

After leaving *egg,* I had made a promise to continue to develop myself. I did not want all that good training and information I had gained there to go to waste, so I began to buy books. It was about that time that I discovered Tony Robbins. Tony is one of the leading personal development gurus in the world; he has sold millions of books, run seminars attended by hundreds of thousands of people and coached some of the most successful people in the world. One night I was watching mind numbing late night TV, when a commercial came on for Personal Power II – Tony's latest home study course. It was a 30-day programme with audio CDs, a workbook and a bunch of bonus tapes, too. In the commercial, Tony shared his personal story and explained how this programme could help me achieve better results in my life. I had always been wary of TV shopping channels; the only thing I had ever bought was some contraption that was supposed to give me a six-pack. However, there was something about the way that Tony spoke. He opened up a world of possibility and made me believe that I could be so much more. I made the order and I was overcome with excitement...I could not wait to get going.

About 2 weeks later the package arrived. I opened the packing immediately and put in the first CD. I was blown away by what I was hearing, and in no time, I was already on to CD 7. I was setting goals, exploring my emotions and creating affirmations. The bottom line was that I was feeling great and I began to see more of the positives in my life. I began to embrace the idea that I was capable of much more. Therefore, the more I learnt, the more my horizons were opened, which would ultimately lead to so much more.

I do not know if it is the Indian blood in me, but I was compelled to start my own business. I figured that with all my experience at *egg. com* I could help other organisations to deliver better customer service and increase sales. At the time, *egg.com* was still seen as a success and I thought that would stand me in good stead. I started to put plans together and then the world changed. The Twin Towers in New York were brought crashing down by terrorists and the world was shaken. World Markets crashed and economies took a beating as millions were wiped off the stock exchanges across the world. It was the worst time for me to be starting a business I thought. Instead, I began applying for jobs; I had plenty of experience, so I thought I would not have too much trouble. Boy was I wrong!

In a 6-month period, I must have applied for over 100 jobs. I had rejection after rejection. I was told I had too much experience; I was told there were other candidates better equipped than I, and most of the time I was just told, "you have been unsuccessful on this occasion" with no further explanation. One prospective employer even told me that he felt I would get bored in the role and leave his company! As my redundancy money began to run out, I became more and more desperate. I remember on one occasion after taking yet another rejection phone call, I just dropped to my knees and sobbed. *Was I really this worthless? Why would no one give me a chance?*, I asked myself. I started to come up with all sorts of reasons, such as the colour of my skin, or ridiculously that the training *egg* gave me, had turned me into a square peg in a round hole...I even blamed Tony Robbins and all the positive thinking stuff. I wished I could have forgotten all the information that I had learned and just be like a normal employee.

I was at my lowest point...I cannot tell you some of the thoughts that crossed my mind, but my obligation to my family kept me from doing something stupid. One particular day, I was having an especially bad time and just could not get motivated to do anything. I sat in my chair in the study staring at the wall when I heard Tony's voice in my head. He said: "Parmar, what on earth are you doing? What are you focusing on?" You see one of Tony's key lessons was that energy flows where your focus goes. I had become so caught up in the downward spiral of rejection and focused on all the setbacks that I was creating a negative energy and that was good for nobody – especially me. He reminded me that 'events were just events' but it was the meaning that I gave to them which drove my emotions – which in turn would drive my actions. I sat still and allowed that thought to absorb into my body. Damn it! *Tony you are right; what the hell am I doing?*, I proclaimed. It was time to stand tall.

I had stopped listening to audio CDs and reading books. I had paid far too much attention to the news and all the gloom that was being reported. Instantly I began to focus my attention on the positives, I put all my rejection letters out of sight and began to make a list of all my positive attributes. I repeated them to myself each day with conviction and confidence.

I took some time but I emerged from underneath that dark cloud with a new sense of possibility. Sometimes we need to remember that it is darkest right before the dawn. Within a couple of weeks, I landed a new job; it was not exactly what I wanted and it was some distance from my home, but the goal was to put food on the table and pay the bills. It was not all bad; I found my confidence growing stronger as I was able to put my skills and experience to good use. I followed my natural instinct to network within the company and developed some good relationships. Eventually, another opportunity came my way when I learned about a position at an outsourcing company that was running a project for *egg*. I was delighted to get it, as I had always wanted to get back into *egg* but there was never the right opportunity, even though it was not working directly for them it would get me close enough to where I wanted to be.

In 2003, after 14 months of job satisfaction, I eventually achieved my goal of getting back into *egg*. Finally, I was no longer a square peg in a round hole, I felt like I was going home. I know that may sound ridiculous, but you have to understand the impact that working at *egg* had on me – it was more than just a job.

In no time, I was into the swing of things again. I was the happiest I had been for a long time, and finally making my mark again. Jem and I had been married now for three years, and as such, we began to talk about starting a family. However, there were other motivating factors that had made us come to this decision; aside from my happy demeanour, Jem held a belief that she needed to be a mother before she reached thirty years old, and was tired of people asking her when we were going to start a family.

In our culture, there is an expectation that once you get married that children will follow soon after. Despite the fact that that belief has died down a little over the years, it is still ingrained to some degree in Indian culture, because family are so important. Every function we would go to we were asked "No kids yet?" "How long have you guys been married?" followed by "Don't leave it too long..." It was not for lack of trying; however, after a couple of years thereafter – nothing was happening. Soap Operas have you believe that it is easy to get pregnant; to get drunk, go to a party, sleep with some one – and hey presto! – you're done!

We tried all sorts of traditional Indian treatments; we prayed all the time, and even made regular fasts as a sacrifice to God. Eventually, Jem suggested we go and see the doctor. At first, I was not keen, and looking back on it now there was a male ego thing going on there. I found it hard to accept that something might be wrong with me. Jem is a skilled negotiator and after a series of discussions, she finally got her way, so I agreed to go and see the doctor. After some personal questions and some pressure, the doctor referred her to a fertility specialist.

After the initial meeting, we underwent some tests to identify the root cause. Jem was more anxious than I was to find out what was going on; it was not that I did not care; it was just that I had a more relaxed attitude about how quickly this should happen.

We went back for the test results and we were both really disappointed. The verdict was that everything was in order and our inability to get pregnant was unknown. That was not very helpful as you can imagine. The specialist laid out the options; we were able to get on treatment plan called IUI (a kind of artificial insemination) and if that did not work, we would have one shot at IVF on the NHS.

So that was that! The wheels were set in motion – just as our marriage had been facilitated – may be our pregnancy would be, too...

Chapter Nine – Double Trouble

Although there was now a ray of hope in terms of getting pregnant and having a baby, I was still feeling a little apprehensive about the whole thing – to be more accurate – I was feeling inadequate. So many of the other people I knew who were married around the same time or after us had already started families, some were even on their second or third child. It seemed to me that there were some people in the world, who just had to think about getting pregnant, and magically the Universe would deliver.

Every time Jem and I heard about babies being abandoned or some teenager getting pregnant by accident, it inevitably broke our hearts. *Why would the Universe bless these people with a child and not two people who would love it so much?*

Naturally, we did not broadcast the fact that we were having treatment to help us get pregnant. I did not even tell my Dad for two reasons: one, because no matter how old you are there is still something uncomfortable about discussing anything to do with the birds and the bees, and secondly, because I was still a little embarrassed by the whole thing. None of the other men in our extended family seemed to have problems in becoming a father, so what the hell was wrong with me? Jem on the other hand was focussed on what we had to do and much more positive about the process. In the same way that I had questions about my manhood, I guess she saw having a baby as sign of her womanhood.

The IUI process takes something that should be so natural and turns it into a mechanical cold process. The first part involves administering a series of injections, which stimulate egg production. You are given a kit bag, which contains syringe casings and needles, along with an automated injector and some kind of needle disposal. Then there are the drugs, which come in powder form and need to be mixed to a strict concentration. Some of the drugs even need to be kept in the fridge. Along with the injections came regular visits to the hospital to scan for the number of eggs produced and the size, to predict the optimum time for insemination.

Thankfully, we had a four opportunities funded by the NHS, so going into our first stage of treatment, the pressure was not quite as intense as it may have been. We began the first cycle carefully following the instructions we had been given. I was in charge of administering the injections and mixing up the drugs. The first time I gave Jem the injection I was shaking life a leaf. I know my Mom had dreams of me becoming a doctor, but this was ridiculous!

A few days in, we were due for the first set of scans to assess the egg production. For some reason these were always first thing in the morning and unfortunately Jem is not a morning person, so you can imagine for yourself the cursing that came out of her mouth before every appointment.

On the second visit, the consultant declared that everything was perfect and we were all systems go for the next step. A final injection was to be given to release the eggs, and then it would be time to visit the hospital for the conclusion of the process. Of course, this was not just about Jem and her eggs; I had a vital part to play, too. I had to provide the other magic ingredient – Sperm! I was given a tub and asked to make a deposit. At first, the tub appeared to be the size of a jam jar. The instructions said that I was to receive no assistance in producing the deposit and that during transport, I was to keep the tub upright at all times. I found a whole new use for the cup holder in my car. On arrival at the hospital, I had to take the deposit up to a lab so they could wash it and ensure only the finest of the soldiers were left for the final mission. The lab had Fort Knox-like security. I had to announce my visit via intercom and wait for the door to release. At the top of the stairs was another layer of security and I was further scrutinized by the lady assistant, who checked and double checked that I was who I said I was and that I was on the list for the day. I happened to notice that all the staff at the lab were women, which just added to the embarrassment factor. There was another man waiting with his deposit hand, too; we just gave each other an awkward polite nod as if to say, "Hey, what's up?" and totally ignoring what we knew we had in our hands.

After a few hours, the sperm was washed and ready for collection. Again there was the cross checking to ensure that what was given back to me was indeed mine. It was reassuring that so much care was taken, as the thought had entered my mind as to what would happened if deposits got mixed up.

For the final leg of the journey, we were taken to a private room where the insemination took place. It took all of 30 seconds. We were left alone for a few minutes; we then looked at each other with a glint of hope in our eyes, knowing that in a few days, we could be celebrating.

Friends of ours had been telling us for ages that we needed a holiday to relax us and therefore we booked some time away to Florida. The day before we flew, it seemed that Mother Nature paid Jem a visit – she had a bleed. Unfortunately, it seemed the process had not worked this time. She was devastated. I was devastated, but I tried to make light of it by focussing on the fact that we had three more attempts and joking that "we did not really expect it to work the first time" – or did we?

We landed in sunny Florida the next day. We were staying with my uncle, who worked at a motel not far from Daytona Beach. He had emigrated just before my Mom had died and I had not seen him since.

Opposite the motel was an IHOP (International House of Pancakes) where we decided to take breakfast on our first morning. We were both pretty hungry, so Jem ordered a stack of pancakes with what looked like an entire block of butter on top and I had an omelette, which was the size of a small city. As we dug in, we discussed plans for the trip. We decided to do all the amuse-ment parks and also get some time on the beach. About halfway through the conversation Jem began to look a little pale, and she said she was feeling sick. I suggested we go out and get some air. As the fresh air hit her, she headed toward a dumpster to be sick. A few moments later, she was sick again. It was unlike her and I was sure that the catering at IHOP was not that bad, so next the idea was to get her back to the room and lie down for a while. Back in the room, she was sick again. We could not work out why she was feeling like this and then it hit her. Jem said that since the visit from Mother Nature a couple days earlier, there had been no further signs; we both looked at each other for moment, with neither of us daring to say it aloud but both knowing what the other was thinking. Then she said it: "I wonder if I am pregnant?"

"There is only one way to find out," I said. "We need to take a preg-nancy test!" I exclaimed.

We were supposed to be heading to one of the Disney parks later that morning with my cousins and thought the best plan would be to stop by a store on the way home. All the time we were there we kept smiling to our-selves and whispering to each other, as we could not hold the anticipation in – my cousins must had thought we were crazy.

We stopped at a Walgreens Pharmacy and we bought a dozen test kits from different brands. We convinced my cousins to wait outside in the car, as we did not want them to see what we were doing.

The 5-minute drive from the store to the motel seemed like an age. Once back at the motel I cannot even remember what excuse we made but we headed straight to our room. We tore open the boxes and began to try each test...we tried each test twice and each time we got the same result... POSITIVE, POSITIVE, POSITIVE!

We could not believe it. It had worked...we were pregnant. After all those years finally, the eagle had landed! We jumped up and down on the bed like children, and after finally composing ourselves, we headed to my uncle's room to have dinner. We both had to play our best poker face for the remainder of the holiday.

Upon return to the UK, we made an appointment with our GP to confirm the result. We did not say anything to anyone until a further few weeks. Jem's morning sickness was quite bad and, as my Dad lived with us, he was naturally getting a little worried about her. We broke the news to him and he was over the moon; it was as if someone had just walked into the dark room he was in and switched on the brightest light. It felt great to be finally able to give him some great news. He never did or said anything to suggest it but I knew inside that he was hoping for grandchildren. We told our immediate family but agreed that we would not tell anyone else until we had the first scan and we knew that everything was OK.

The first scan date arrived in a flash. We were both nervous; however, at the same time, we were naturally excited. Whether it was a sign of my own nervousness or something entirely different, I was in one of those situations where you say something without having any knowledge why you said it. As we walked into the Sonographer's office, I turned to Jem and said: "Wouldn't it be funny if it was twins?"

She looked at me as only a wife could and replied: "No, I do not think so...I would have to carry them!"

As the Sonographer did her stuff, I sat looking up at the monitor above Jem for any sign of a baby. The Sonographer moved the scanner left and right, the sound of the scanner breaking the silence, and then she made some notes. She then began to describe what she could see. "There is the baby," she said pointing at the monitor. I could not see what she was seeing but just nodded in approval. I had a grin from ear to ear, at which point the Sonographer said: "And there is the other one!"

"Err?! What did you say? Can you say that again please?" I asked.

"Oh, did you not know it was twins?" Jem and I both burst into a fit of laughter. Her words had caused Jem and I to erupt into a fit of laughter – we were out of control – much to the disapproval of the Sonographer, as she endeavoured to complete the tests.

We were absolutely overjoyed with the news. We were told about the increased risks but we did not really care too much about that...we were having TWINS!

During the drive home, I called my Dad to tell him. "You will never guess what, Dad," I said. "We are having twins!" I revealed. He was blown away and at first, he could not believe it. We had similar reactions from both our immediate families. There was a sense of joy that gripped our family that had not been present for a long time. Gradually, as Jem began to show, we started to tell people. Everyone we knew was so happy for us. They told us how much we deserved this, after everything we had been through.

As the reality of it all hit us both, we started to address the practicalities. I had started to make enquires about changing my company car to a bigger one; we started to plan what we would do with the nursery, and then we began researching what life would like with twins through online forums. Although we had no great cause for concern at this point, we were careful not to get too carried away and resisted the urge to go 'baby shopping crazy'.

Then, one cold evening in January 2006, about 19 weeks into the pregnancy, everything was about to change. In the early hours of the morning, Jem could feel that something was not right and, upon further inspection, it looked as if the part of the amniotic sac had come through. We called for an ambulance and we were rushed to Birmingham Heartlands Hospital. The maternity ward was right across from the building where my Mom has passed away years earlier. As we had arrived in the early hours, there were not many doctors about and we had to wait around for a long time before anyone came to attend to us.

The first consultant took one look, and as we had feared, confirmed that little could be done to save the babies. That verdict hit us both like a sledgehammer. Reduced to tears, I looked up towards the 'big man' in the sky and asked what I had done to have been dealt such a bad hand yet again.

Left alone, we comforted each other and made a decision that neither one of us would accept that outcome until it was confirmed. The next doctor to see us suggested that they could try a procedure where they would attempt to push the sac back up into the womb and put a stitch into the cervix to add reinforcement. It was not without risk and there was a possibility it would not work; however, with that there was also a possibility it would work. Jem and I chose to focus on that positive. We had already been waiting for some hours before Jem was prepped for theatre. I had called my family and my in-laws, who had all now arrived at the hospital.

We waited patiently in the lobby area. I was slumped in a chair, praying that this would work. Each time the double doors to the restricted theatre area swung open, I would sit up like a Meerkat surveying his manor. Finally, the surgeon emerged. I could see from his body language that it was not good news. I rushed over to him and he just shook his head and apologised. He said that the sac had ruptured during the procedure and this would put both Jem and the babies at high risk of infection.

Jem was still out under the effects of the anaesthetic and I waited by her side for her to regain consciousness. Although she was not anywhere near the kind of condition my Mom had been in, seeing her hooked up to a drip, heart monitor and other gizmos triggered flashbacks. As she came around a few minutes later, the first thing she asked was if the procedure had worked. Still groggy from the effects of the anaesthetic she could tell from my face that it had not.

The prognosis was that the twins would arrive early, too early for any medical intervention. They would have to reach 24 weeks gestation, which was some 6 weeks away.

It seemed so cruel that a matter of weeks could make such a difference. In our everyday lives, time would fly by without event. Furthermore, neither of us could come to terms with why we had to lose both twins, when only one sac had ruptured.

When I went home that night, I could not get over the feeling of hopelessness. I wished there was something I could do. I was so used to being able to do something to fix things that I was having a hard time accepting what was going on. Right then I had a brain wave and I started to search the internet for cases similar to ours in the hope that I may find information that could help us. Sure enough, I found articles in American medical journals and other publications, which gave me more insight. I read that increasing the fluid intake could replenish fluid around the baby in the absence of the sac.

Willing to do anything, Jem began to drink more water. It seemed from the regular scans we were having that something was working. Our consultant was even surprised. Two weeks in, we were still going against the odds. Even when a senior consultant told us the odds were stacked firmly against us, Jem and I both clung on to hope with both hands.

On the 4th February, the hope was to be snatched away from us. The umbilical cord of the twin whose sac had ruptured came through, and the doctors felt there was too greater risk to Jem to wait any longer.

That night Jem went into an induced labour. As the contractions got closer, the nursing staff warned us that the twins may be born alive and reminded us that they would not be able to resuscitate or offer any medical assistance.

At approximately 7.20 a.m. the twins were born. A boy and a girl. I was surprised at how developed they were, with perfectly formed tiny hands and feet. The boy was stillborn, but looked very much like me — he had my ears and nose. The little girl was born alive and had features like Jem. Her little chest was pumping away as she fought for her life. I just held her in the palm of my hand. She was tiny. I looked over at the nurses and asked how long she would keep going; they expected her to stop breathing within minutes.

Over an hour later her heart was still beating...it had slowed considerably but it was still going. That made an important difference. Because she had survived for over an hour she was no longer classed a neonatal death, and instead, was classified as an infant death. What that meant was we would have to register her birth, therefore etching her name into history. We named her Ria Parmar and although we did not have to, we named her brother, Ryan.

The experience for both of us was devastating. I think for Jem it was so much more, as she gave birth, and yet there was no baby for her to hold in her arms. The following months were some of the most difficult of our lives. Losing my Mom had been more my loss than Jem's, but this was the first loss we had both experienced fully together. I think it was the loss we had shared, which ultimately was to bring us much closer together.

As is our custom with children who pass before bearing teeth, both babies were buried at a local cemetery. From time to time when I feel lost or need to find some strength, I visit their grave and think about the fighting spirit that Ria had showed in her short but impactful life. She is a constant source of inspiration — a reminder of hope — and of human possibility.

Chapter Ten – The Gift and the Curse

Losing the twins was another slap in the face, a harsh reminder that life can change so quickly. One minute you can be on a high and the next you are back down – down in the depths of despair – such is the game of life.

Each time we heard news of friends or family getting pregnant, we were torn between feeling happy for them, and yet at the same time, feeling resentment. We avoided going to see family with young children, baby showers and any other event where there was the possibility of babies being present. On reflection, it was a ridiculous strategy but at the time, it was what we needed to do to maintain our overall sanity.

We decided to get away to clear our heads. We headed to India. I had been before but always to see family so had never been able to travel freely. Seizing the opportunity with both hands, we put together a tour, which would include a visit to the magical Taj Mahal, the historic city of Jaipur and the beautiful planes of Rajasthan. We also included a trip to Sri Lanka, where we would visit an elephant orphanage before we headed over to the Maldives for some real relaxation ahead of the trip home. We invited Atul, Sheema and their kids along with us for some company, and to keep our spirits up. My mother-in-law had been a rock for Jem, taking care of her and supporting me, too, so to thank her, we thought it would be only right to take her with us.

My previous trips to India had been fun but this was different. Even though I was born and bred in England, it felt like a homecoming. I felt a real sense of connection, as if my spiritual soul was being cleansed. The pain from the loss of the twins was still raw but in the process of rediscovery, my spirituality found peace with what had happened.

At the same time, I had a kind of awakening. I had slipped back into the corporate hamster wheel and become too comfortable. That desire I had to "change the world" after my Mom's death had faded. I figured that the loss of the twins was a signal to reignite that passion to make my mark on the world by making a real difference.

As luck would have it, at that time *egg* was going through some major changes including a restructure. I found myself being made redundant again; however, this time it was what I wanted. I had learnt my lesson from the last time and had already begun working on plans months beforehand, lining things up. My piece of consultancy work started a week or two after *egg* had let me go. I was working as an associate trainer for an established consultancy, which worked well for me. I was paid to deliver content I was passionate about and was therefore able to sharpen my skills.

Meanwhile, Jem was ready to begin another cycle of treatment. It was only a few months since losing the twins and to be honest, I was worried about the impact on her health and the long-term effects of the drugs she would have to take. She was adamant that the treatment should continue, and so we gave it another shot.

Our luck was in...it was successful again. This time the doctors decided that they would give us an early scan to check things out. The 8-week scan showed everything to be OK, which was a relief to us, but we were still cautious and decided not to tell anyone the news. It was only at 16 weeks, and just before the next scan that we told our close family. After the sadness that had followed losing the twins, everyone was now so happy for us that we finally had something to celebrate...but no one knew what was about to happen.

The morning of 14th January, we headed to the hospital tingling with anticipation and a dash of apprehension. There we were again, this time there was no comment about twins. In fact, I was very quiet for a change. The sonographer invited us in to her office; she had our file in her hand, which had a sticker on it, warning her that we had lost a baby previously.

As usual, she prepped Jem with some gel on her stomach and began to scan. I remember that she moved slowly, she was not as chatty as last time. Jem and I were just fixated on the monitor where we were trying to make out the baby in amongst the shades of grey. Oddly, the sonographer left the office for a few minutes, and when she returned, there was something different about her demeanour. She turned to us, took a deep breath and said, "I am really sorry Mr and Mrs Parmar, but there is a serious problem with the baby's development." She had been to see one of the specialists, as she had found that the baby's nervous system and skull had not formed correctly.

All I can remember from that moment on was Jem turning to me crying and yelling, "Oh no, not again!"

The recommendation was to terminate the pregnancy. It sounded like we had a choice but in reality, there was no choice, as the baby would die naturally within a few days.

I made a few phone calls to tell the family the bad news, before we were whisked away to have the procedure done. It was all too familiar, the same suite, the same ward and some of the same nurses. In fact, one of the nurses saw me walking around and recognised me from last time. She assumed we were on ward because we were pregnant again and when I told what happened she was devastated. She came straight through to see Jem and to comfort her.

Throughout both experiences, the nursing staff on the ward was fabulous. We could not have asked for a better quality of care and for that, we will always be grateful.

I just could not believe this could happen again. I remember the words of Bruce Willis in Die Hard 2: "How can the same shit happen to the same guy twice?" The reasons for both losses were unrelated; we were just the victims of a horrible coincidence. *How we would move on from this?* I had no idea.

Jem and I had a long chat and we agreed to stay off any further treatment for at least 12 months. I had read about the long-term effects of fertility drugs and I was also becoming increasingly worried about the impact on her well-being. Instead we left it to fate...if this was meant to be, then it would be. Jem's patience with fate wore thin and soon we were back on the treatment wheel but this time we had no luck, both remaining attempts failed. The only option left was full IVF and we would only get one attempt on the NHS.

In 2009, during an IVF briefing session, we were given all kinds of statistics. The chance of success seemed so low compared to the inherent risks. I never knew that there was a risk of death during the IVF process. Having a baby was important to me but not as much as having Jem in my life. If there was an increased risk to her, then I was not prepared to go with it; however, Jem was determined to exhaust every avenue – and as another door was about to open – it was one that neither of us ever expected.

My phone rang and it was Jem's brother Atul; he wanted to discuss something with us and asked us to come over. We are a close-knit family. They have three children who are like our adopted kids and we spend a lot of time together, so we did not think that there was anything peculiar about his request. However, nothing could have prepared us for what he had to tell us...

"We are expecting another baby," he said. We were delighted for them, but before we could begin to congratulate them, he said, "But there is something we need to tell you. We really hadn't planned for this. We don't have the room and at the moment we cannot afford another baby

– financially we just cannot support another child – and we don't want to... err...you know...have a...err," he explained.

Then followed the question that we never expected in a million years. "So, we were wondering if you would adopt the baby?" At that point, I am sure my jaw hit the ground.

There was a stunned silence. *How do you answer a question like that?*

As easy as it would have been to, we did not say yes straight away. We said we would think about it and that's what we did. On one level, it seemed perfect – on another, it just seemed very odd. After immediate romance of the idea, all the potential pitfalls came through. *What would happen when the baby was older? How would the baby react? How would my family take this? How would this even work?*

The drive home was very quiet. Jem and I hardly spoke a word to each other as we sat contemplating and processing what we had just been asked to do.

We were taking on a huge responsibility here. Furthermore, there was no guarantee that it would not end in tears.

After about a week of talking about little else, we decided to go for it. We had run through all sorts of scenarios and we spoke to my Dad, who gave us his blessing and full support. As apprehensive as we may have been, in the end, we could not find a reason strong enough in order not to do it.

We called them to give them the news. It was joy all round, as well as a sense of relief. We made it clear from the very beginning that we wanted them to continue to be an integral part of the child's life. Since we spent so much time together and because of our special relationship with the other kids, it would be hard not to have it that way. We also wanted to assure them that if for whatever reason things changed and they no longer wanted to go ahead as agreed, then we would understand.

They had a discussion with the kids to explain what was going to happen with the baby. They asked some great questions; the one that I think struck Sheema the most was when Anisha, her eldest child, asked: "Mummy, how will you feel afterwards?" The answer was that she did not know...none of us would know until it actually happened.

At the same time, my youngest brother Ricky and his wife Kaushika were also expecting their first child. They had married the year before and were living with us whilst they looked for their own place. It was odd knowing that we were all about to become parents but in very different ways. Whilst they were fully immersed and experiencing the developments of pregnancy first hand, Jem and I were regularly in Leicester, attending the scans and appointments for our baby...more like third-party observers.

It is only a little thing but when I used to watch my brother put his hand on his wife's stomach to feel the kick of the baby, I would often wonder what it felt like, emotionally. When we were expecting the twins, Jem had reached the stage where she could feel movement inside, but I never experienced feeling the baby from outside.

Do not misunderstand me; throughout the whole pregnancy, we were involved in all the key decisions and events. We were at all the scans and I was present when we found out the sex of the baby – we were having a girl – we did not tell anyone.

I had not seen Jem this happy for a long time. It was a joy to see the smile on her face. I was happy, too, but in the back of my mind, I always held the possibility that maybe, just maybe Sheema would change her mind. For me, I could not really be fully relaxed until they baby was finally with us.

As the due date drew nearer, we prepared for the arrival. I have a real hatred of decorating; normally Jem would have to nag me for months or sometimes years to get things done. It was a real surprise to her when I managed to get the nursery done in one day!

I had that sense of purpose once again.

My brother's baby was due just 2 weeks before ours. So when baby Aaron arrived, the reality of what was about to happen began to set in. At Aaron's naming ceremony, I watched, as my brother and his wife were full of pride; I could not help but to look forward to my turn in a just a few days time.

Our baby's due date was 12th August, which came and went without incident. I am sure that Sheema would have been fed up with us calling her every few hours asking if there was any sign. Bless her, she was so patient and polite about the whole thing, anyone else would have taken the phone off the hook!

As the 13th came and went, too, Jem and I decided to head to Leicester, as it was the weekend and we figured the baby would be due any day now. Before we went I decided that I would tell my brothers that we were due to have girl and shared the list of names Jem and I had compiled. Normally in my culture, names are given depending on star sign and, since the star sign changes each hour, there is no way of predicting it. Jem wanted to stick to tradition; I on the other hand, was less attached to the idea.

I think that the names we selected went down very well – I really like Ella. Much in the same way I had made the comment about twins, my brother Dipit's wife Rita, suggested the name India.

Fate was to take the lead, because at 7.28 a.m. on 15th August, which happened to be India's Independence Day, little India Tara Parmar was born, weighing in at a healthy 8lbs.

Perhaps just to make up for all the bad cards we had been dealt before, the 'big man' made sure that she bonded with Jem (who was Sheema's birthing partner) first. India was born with a low temperature and therefore in order to keep her warm, the nurse asked Jem to put India inside her T-shirt, which meant that was her first skin-to-skin contact.

I was not allowed in the delivery suite, and so I waited patiently outside. Eventually, Atul emerged with tears in his eyes as he broke the news to me. There are not any words to describe what I was feeling at that time, other than I felt as if I was 10 ft high and that I could walk on water.

Chapter Eleven – The Home Coming

Coming face to face with India for the first time was the most nervous I have ever felt in my entire life. I have stood in front of hundreds of people and delivered speeches and never felt anywhere near the kind of butterflies that were flying around my stomach at that moment. My self-talk was doing overtime – How would she react to me? *What if she rejected me? What if she hated me?*

My heart accelerated as I approached the cot she lay in, and for several seconds, I just stood looking in awe at this beautiful baby. I then reached into the cot to pick her up for the first time, and as I drew her closer to me, my fears instantly disappeared because it all felt so natural to me. I had feared that it would be like holding someone else's baby; however, in that moment, I could not have felt more connected with her, she felt like my own child – she belonged to me – and I belonged to her. I extended my finger and offered it to her; as her tiny hand grasped it tightly, I gently whispered into her ear: "Hey, India. It's Daddy; you are so beautiful." I had waited what seemed like an eternity to say those words – to be able to say "It's Daddy" – was incredible.

India was released from hospital that evening after her temperature had recovered back to normal levels. We had planned to stay in Leicester the first night India was born so that Sheema, Atul and the kids would get some time with her, and it was important to us that they had some time to adjust; it would not have been right to just up and leave.

Lots of family and friends came to visit us at Atul's home, in which they congratulated us for becoming parents. It was a surreal moment for Jem and me, as neither of us could actually believe that we were being referred to as parents; it felt as if we were in some kind of dream and that any moment we would wake up. We sat in awe as we watched Sheema switch straight into *auntie mode*; all the while, she held her smile, referring to herself as *'Mami'*, which is the Gujarati word for maternal aunt. She held her distance so as not to encroach on our moment, not that she would have ever been seen as intruding – not for a single moment, as she had given an enormous sacrifice – a gift that was well beyond our comprehension. In one single, selfless act, she had injected our lives with a lifetime of happiness, one that she will never fully comprehend.

Our first night as Mommy and Daddy was interesting. We had been preparing for a sleepless night, but not in the way we had imagined. It was not India getting up that kept us awake; in fact, amazingly she slept through, but we kept getting up to check she was OK. I lost count of the amount of times I checked to see if she was breathing! There was one moment when I suddenly woke up in panic because I thought I had slept for hours and missed India crying...but she was fast asleep, with not a care in the world.

Eventually, we were woken by India's call for food at 4 a.m., and from that point onwards, normal service was resumed.

On the afternoon of August 16th, we prepared to leave Leicester for home. A ritual was performed, which provided blessings for the official handing over of India to Jem and me. As Sheema placed India into Jem's lap, the first visible signs of what an emotional impact this would have appeared, as tears streamed from both their eyes. That was the first time I saw Sheema and Atul visibly upset.

We strapped India into her car seat and finally we were able to say our goodbyes. It was inevitable that we would all shed tears during what was an intensely emotional time for us all – one of joy – and yet one of sorrow for Atul and Sheema. As we drove off, I glanced through the rear-view mirror and watched them embrace, as they were finally able to express their emotions without worrying about upsetting us.

I do not think the journey from Leicester to Birmingham has ever taken us quite as long as it did that day. It was the most cautious and reserved I think I have ever been behind the wheel. I guess the responsibility of fatherhood had begun to take its hold on me.

We arrived home with the sun beaming down, it seemed fitting as we were bringing a new ray of sunshine home. Emotions were high as traditionally my Mom would have greeted us and carried out rituals, and even after such a long time, I found I really missed her. Before I got married, she often talked about looking forward to having grandchildren, how she would spoil them, where she would take them and how she would give up work to look after them. She would have been so proud; I could just imagine the smile on her face.

In Gujarati tradition, the naming ceremony called the 'Chatti' takes place on the sixth day of a child's life. It is the first real religious ceremony in a Hindu's life and it is another family occasion. We invited my mother-in-law, Atul, Sheema and the kids along with other close family members and friends to share in this most significant of moments. It was particularly significant because it would be the first time that many of my side of the family would meet India and accept her into our clan.

The following months were amazing yet challenging. Business was proving difficult, as it was not moving in the direction that I wanted it to; in fact, it was not moving at all and had ground to a halt. However, I was able to play a very active part in bringing up India at home – as a *stay at home Dad*. I would cherish the moments when I would sit with her, and she would lie sleeping on my chest. I would adjust my breathing in an attempt to stay in tandem with her, while regularly kissing the top of her head.

Those early months were full of amazing moments – moments that I never thought I would experience – her first smile, her first attempt at crawling, and her very first Christmas.

Although India was living with us, we had yet to complete the official adoption process. All the while that was pending, there was a niggling fear in the back of my mind that India would be taken away from us. I know it might sound ridiculous now, but with all that had happened in my life, I did not think it was beyond the realm of possibility.

The stress of trying to make the business work, the increasing financial pressures and the pending legal process were all playing havoc with my emotions. I was becoming more and more desperate to preserve the illusion that everything was OK and that I could handle the heat. When asked how business was at my regular breakfast networking meetings or family functions, I would lie and tell people everything was great. I felt more and more like a fraud and became resentful of the person I was becoming. It was then that I met up with my coach and good friend Paul Harris for what would turn out to be another critical turning point in my life.

We sat round his dining table where I looked him in the whites of his eyes and declared that I could not carry on anymore. It was time to come clean, step forward, and face the music. Admitting to myself that I was failing, was difficult. I was such a positive person and seen as such by so many others that I felt I'd be letting them down. Just then, Paul said something to me that changed my perspective. "You've got to put your own oxygen mask on first, before you can help others," he said in his usual matter-of-fact way. He was right. How could I expect to help others, if I was not able to breathe myself?

While setting out a practical plan to help ease the pressures, there was something else I needed to address, which I knew would help me breathe better. I needed to strengthen my relationship with God.

Although I had never completely lost my faith in God, our relationship had – well – it had become strained. We only seemed to talk when I needed something from Him or He needed something from me. I was born a Hindu and as such, I just followed where my parents and community guided me, but if I was to really develop my relationship with God I needed to find my own answers.

I started a simple practice of daily prayer where I did not ask for anything but instead thanked the Universe for everything I already had. I rediscovered my love for reading, and it was through studying the work of Mahatma Gandhi in the book *A higher standard of leadership* that I made an important discovery and ultimately found greater spiritual connection. There were a number of practices, which the author, Keshavan Nair, drew out but it was the practice of personal service, which I found particularly inspiring.

In my study of personal development, I had often come across the notion that if you help other people get what they want, then you will get what you want. I was always a little uncomfortable with that, as it suggested that there had to be something to be gained in order for you to serve. However, this book talked about serving your fellow human being because it was the right thing to do.

I began to give my time and energy to projects unconditionally, especially where there was no chance of personal gain for me. Some people may read that and conclude that this was a stupid strategy. Even though it did little for me financially, I felt a sense of fulfilment and personal satisfaction, which helped me to reveal the real me. The trouble I had always had about trying to fit in or find my place in the world began to fade. I was finally becoming completely comfortable in my own skin.

Every moment I was with India demanded that I was *me and only me*. I did not need to put on a front, pretend to be strong or hide any feelings.

The more I got comfortable with *me*, the more the fog lifted and I could finally see what I needed to do clearly.

Within a few weeks, I picked up some contract work and almost simultaneously, the legal process around India's adoption suddenly speeded up.

The adoption process involved being screened by Social Services. It is fair to say that Social Services did not always enjoy positive press coverage and so ahead of our first meeting we were very anxious about how it would pan out. *What kind of details would they want to go into? What would happen if they did not approve our application?* We need not have been so worried because Liz, our assigned social worker, was brilliant. She put our minds at rest immediately and made everything so easy. There was a thorough process to go through, which included criminal checks, gaining personal references and enduring a series of interviews to ensure that we had considered fully the potential scenarios.

During all this, India's first birthday was coming up. The first year of her life had passed so quickly, we could hardly believe that a year was almost upon us. It was a day that we never thought we would see and with that in mind, we wanted to do something big to celebrate. We decided to hold a party, not just to celebrate India's birthday, but also to thank all the amazing people that had supported us throughout our journey. Jem had decided on a 'Hello Kitty' theme and went to town on the co-ordination of decor, invites and party favours. I was just happy to see her so happy.

The arrival of India had transformed Jem. When she lost the twins, I think a part of her went with them. She had been riddled with guilt at times even though she had done nothing wrong. She was so desperate to be a mother; it had been killing me that I was unable to help her achieve that.

Throughout the party, I watched Jem from afar, as she glided around and greeted people. She was grinning from ear to ear and radiating happiness through every cell in her body. All the tears, the heartbreaks and disappointments were now finally behind her, she now had a little girl who called her Mummy with unrivalled affection. For Jem, the first time India said Mummy was the moment when she felt it really sink in.

As much as I loved India and felt connected to her, it was not until I stood at the cake table in front of all my family and friends singing happy birthday to her, that I felt validated by the Universe as her father. It was almost like a public recognition.

The party was amazing; my mother-in-law had truly out done herself as head chef! Being surrounded by people who genuinely care for you creates such an incredible energy; not only does it make you feel good, but also it keeps you grounded.

Within a couple of months of India's birthday, we found ourselves in Solihull Magistrates Court for the adoption hearing and the official signing of the paperwork. The date of the hearing was November 23rd and the wait was unbearable, so both Liz our social worker and our solicitor Karen did their best to calm us down.

Upon entering the room where the hearing would take place, the formality of the situation suddenly struck me. The panel of judges sat opposite us and as the main judge began to read out their statement, tears began to stream from Jem's face closely followed by Atul, who wept with emotion. It is a bit of family joke, the Gohil water works, one of them cries and it sets them all off!

The judges were moved by our story, having no doubt that the situation we were in was indeed, the best for India. With that, they approved the paperwork, which I followed with a reserved cry of "Yes!", as I was exploding with happiness. Finally, it was done and we felt complete; as Stevie Wonder once sang: "Signed, Sealed, Delivered", India was now ours!

We know that this is by no means the end; in fact, it is just the beginning of the next stage of our journey. We all know that the road ahead is unpredictable and there will be some tough times in front of us. However, all we can do is focus on now and shower India with all the love and affection we can find; she has been the magical ingredient in our lives since she arrived in 2010.

We are often asked how we think she will react to us when she discovers that we are not her birth parents – the answer is that we just do not know. We hope that she will understand what a special child she is and that Atul and Sheema love her just as much as Jem and I love her. We hope that she will grow up to understand what she represents, not just to us, but also to all those who hear her story. She represents hope, possibility and unconditional love, all of which is needed in abundance in this crazy world we live in.

I hope that one day, India is able to sit with her children or even grandchildren and able to share the incredible story that she was part of – a legacy that will inspire generations to come in our families.

THE 7 PRINCIPLES OF BOUNCE-BACK-ABILITY

The powerful principles I discovered for dealing with change and adversity.

Introduction

The purpose of writing this book was not only to share my story, but in the hope that it will inspire those who read it, to understand that no matter what happens in life, you can always come back stronger. As I am sure you can imagine, along my journey I have learned some important lessons, received sound advice and made critical changes to my mindset, which enabled me to get through and rise above the challenges that I faced.

What I learned was that dealing with challenge, change or adversity that it is an inner game, which is played out in our minds. It is all about what we think, what influences our attitude, and how we make decisions in situations where we feel we are up against it. To describe that mix I borrowed a phrase used by a football team manager named Ian Dowie. He famously coined the phrase 'bounce-back-ability' when talking about how his team needed to rise up from their recent defeat and move forward.

In this final chapter, I have pulled together a set of 7 key principles, which I believe have been the key to my success in overcoming challenges and bouncing back stronger. I call them principles rather than rules because they are beliefs to adopt rather than rules to stick to. Furthermore, they should not be viewed as sequential steps, as the order in which you apply them is not critical to their effectiveness. There are various schools of thought, which may challenge or question their validity; however, as one of my teachers Topher Morrison once said: "I don't care if they are true or not; I just like the results I get." At the end of the day, isn't that the most important thing?

I will caution you that some or even all of these principles may challenge your current thinking. I do hope that you will be open enough at least to try them on for size. Just think of it like shopping for clothes – try on each principle, see how it fits – then decide if it is for you. If it is not, you can discard it and continue with what has served you well.

Below are my 7 Principles of Bounce-back-ability – enjoy!

Principle #1 Your Results are defined by your Decisions, not your Conditions.

When things go well in your life, you are there. When you are making more money than you dreamed of, you are there. When your relationship is rock steady, you are there. When you are in the best shape of your life, you are there. You are also there, when things are not going to plan. You are also there, when you are struggling to make ends meet. You are also there, when your relationship is at breaking point and, you are there, when your waist has jumped up a couple of sizes. Notice a pattern here?

That is right; it is YOU. You are always present no matter the circumstances and therefore you are responsible for everything that happens in your life. You are the creator. You can change everything in your life.

Where you are now is the sum total of all the choices you have made – both consciously and unconsciously. I am not suggesting for a minute that you deliberately cause problems in your life or that you purposely set out to do wrong. I am not saying that you are responsible in the context of blame, but what I am saying is that you are responsible for your actions and emotions.

Let me give a personal example, because I know from my own experience that this can be difficult to grasp at first. When I was first introduced to this notion, my reaction was to say to my coach at the time: "Are you saying I am responsible for my Mom's death?"

Of course the answer is no.

I am not responsible for my Mom contracting meningitis and dying on my wedding day but I am responsible for my actions and emotions in relation to that incident. I could wallow in self-pity, be angry at God for taking her and blame all the bad things that have happened in my life on the poor hand that life had dealt me, but where would that leave me? I would always use that incident as an excuse for the results in my life.

It would be more powerful for me to take total responsibility and say, yes my Mom died on my wedding, yes it's painful and yes I miss her dearly, but I choose where I go from here. It is my choice as to how I feel about it and how I live my life. Instead of being angry or blaming my circumstances, I choose to use my learning to take stock of my life and seize the opportunity that life brings.

When you place the responsibility for what happens in your life at someone or something else's feet, you become victim and give away your personal power. Instead, by taking full responsibility and understanding that you are the creator, you have more choices and therefore more personal power.

Remember you are the creator, you are the scriptwriter and you are the only person in your life that can change the results you get.

Principle #2 You see the World the way you see it, not how it is.

Has someone ever recommended you a movie, only to find when you watched it you could not really see what all the fuss was about? Worse still, they thought it was great and you thought it sucked.

Perhaps someone you know got upset by a text message or an email they were sent but when they showed it to you, you could not understand why they felt the way they did?

In both examples you were both looking at the same thing – the movie or the text message – so how it is that you can draw such different conclusions?

We all experience the world in different ways. From the moment we are born (and some people believe before that), we are like a sponge absorbing all the information around us. Everything we see, hear, touch, taste and smell is information coming into our awareness, which enables us to make sense of the world. As we grow, we develop a set of filters, which dictate the level of importance we place on the various bits of information.

These filters are created through the values we adopt, the beliefs we develop and the experiences we go through, which of course are different for each of us. What this means is that we develop a unique model of the world – the world as we see it – not as it is.

Our emotions are created as a result of these filters. What we focus on – what we take notice of – drives our emotions, which then in turn drive our actions, behaviour and paint the picture of the world we see.

It reminds me of a story I once heard about a monk who was greeted by two travellers. The first traveller met the monk on his way from a village he had visited. He looked upset and tired. He stopped to ask the monk how far the next village was to which the monk replied, "There is a village 15 miles ahead." The monk was curious as to why this young man was so upset and asked him what was wrong.

The young man replied, "The people in the last village were so mean, rude and unwelcoming. They wouldn't help me and I couldn't wait to get away from them." He then asked, "What are the people like in the village ahead?"

The monk replied, "I'm afraid that you will find the same there, my son. And it's the last village for over 300 miles." Disappointed and disgruntled the traveller trotted off into the distance.

A couple of days later the monk was greeted by another traveller. He had come from the same village as the previous man. He was happy, smiling and seemed full of energy. "Is there another village ahead?" he asked the monk.

"Yes, 15 miles ahead there is a village. It is the last one for 300 miles."

"What are the people like?" asked the young man.

"What were the people like in the village you just came from?" asked the monk, full of curiosity.

"They were wonderful, so caring and polite. They made me feel so welcome that I really didn't want to leave," explained the traveller.

"You will find the same in the next village," replied the monk. With that, the traveller went on his way with a spring in his step.

When we find ourselves in tough times, we ought to ask ourselves what we are focussing on.

Principle #3 Purpose first – plan second.

When you have been hit with a sucker punch in life, it can be hard to find the motivation to go on. You know in your mind's eye that the show must go on but your heart cannot muster up the motivation to move you forward. Especially, but not exclusively, when you suffer the loss of a loved one.

So how do you begin to move forward? How do you take that next step? Some people believe in setting big goals and making grand plans, which I agree with; however, ask yourself; how many times have you set goals and made plans that have never really come into reality. I believe there is a step before all of the goal setting and plan making, and that is connecting to your purpose. Whereas goals are something we drive towards, purpose is something that pulls us toward it. When we are acting in service of our purpose, it just feels right. People often talk about finding their purpose, but I am of the old school of thought that states that your purpose will find you once your awareness is opened up.

For most of our lives, we live into a synthetic purpose; it is the conditioning we have had to get educated, to work hard, to make money, to pay the bills, etc.

When we suffer a blow in life and something unexpected happens to us, we seem to snap out of that model and begin to question ourselves as to why we should continue. For example, when losing someone you love you may question the value of money. *What's the point of having all this money if I have no one to share it with?* Or, if you are suddenly made redundant, you may think: *What's the point of working so hard and being loyal?*

In order to begin to move forward you need to find a compelling enough reason to continue – a reason 'why', which is bigger than yourself – that is purpose – your authentic purpose. The other interesting thing about purpose is that I believe it is a feeling and that while your actions and the way you serve your purpose may change, the feeling is consistent throughout.

For me, my first sense of purpose came in the form of obligation. When I lost my Mom, I looked around at my family and I felt it was my responsibility to take care of things. I had to make sure that I kept going for their sake – this was bigger than I was.

Once you have that sense of purpose you can begin to set goals and make plans in service of it. For example, at the time of my Mom's death I was traveling a lot, which was eating in to precious family time, so I set a goal to find another job closer to home. I also made plans to move us into a bigger house so that we could all live together. Both concepts only came into my thinking because I was connected to my purpose and they felt like the right thing to do.

Today that sense of purpose has become a personal compass, which has helped me to decide on career moves, business decisions, and life changes.

Principle #4 The Virtue of Patience

When I started working at *egg*, telephone banking was still very much in its infancy. First Direct were the major players and they offered a 24hr, 365-day a year service to their customers. I remember thinking at the time – *Who in their right mind would want to call a bank in the middle of the night?*

How things have changed. We are now truly in a 24/7 world. We would no longer find it odd that shops, banks and restaurants are open all hours. The consequence of all that is that our expectations have changed – we have become what I call immediacy junkies – we want everything now!

Let me give you an example. Think back to a few years ago. If you called a company to place an order for something and they told you it would take 7 days to ship, you would more than likely be willing to accept that. Would you do the same today? I doubt it. In a similar fashion, if you applied for credit and your bank told you it would take 48hrs to make a decision, what would you think? Most people would go elsewhere today.

We have become accustomed to having everything now. Even in our working lives, everything seems to be about immediate results. There are many personal development gurus, who promise instant results, rapid changes and other similar claims. People are sucked in to thinking that there is a silver bullet solution, which will get you results NOW.

Being a child of that culture, one of the hardest lessons I have had to learn is to have patience. It is one of the most important disciplines that I have learned to practice, and it has probably made the biggest difference in my life.

In trying to make my business work, I was pushing myself hard and making demands of people around me, which I thought at the time was the right thing to do. Everything had to be now! Now! Now! What I did not realize was that the harder I pushed – the things that I so desperately wanted to achieve – were pushed further away. The result of which was a vicious circle of frustration.

Tony Robbins often says: "People overestimate what they can accomplish in one year and under estimate what they can do in five." – How right he is.

It really struck me when I heard someone tell me a story about bamboo.

A businessman saw an opportunity in the bamboo market and wanted to set up a plantation so that he could harvest the plant and make lots of money. After finding the best possible site, he sourced the world's best bamboo seeds and had them planted. His team of world-class farmers watered and nurtured the crop for a season but the shoots did not grow more than an inch. The businessman grew frustrated and angry, he demanded more from his farmers telling them to give extra care, add more fertilizer and apply the latest technology, but after the second growing season, the trees still had not sprouted. The businessman grew even more frustrated and fired his farmers to bring a new team in the hope that they would get better results. This cycle went on for four solid years and the businessman had nothing tangible to show for all of his efforts in trying to grow the trees.

Eventually; disappointed, frustrated and angry, he declared that the land was worthless, the seeds he had been sold were of poor quality and left the land to the farmers before heading off to pursue other projects.

Now in their fifth year the Chinese bamboo trees finally began to sprout, growing up to eighty feet in just one growing season!

I am not saying that you should not have goals and plans. I am not saying that you should let go completely and leave it to the Universe. What I am saying is that all great things take time; do not let your impatience and desire for instant results get the better of what could be a lifetime of riches.

Principle #5 Love your Family, choose your Peer Group.

No matter how well you plan or prepare for your journey, somewhere along the line you will face some challenges. The question I want to ask you is whom will you turn to when those situations arise?

Will you turn to your friends and family or your peer group?

Before you answer that, I want to explain the difference.

Your family and friends love you. They want to protect you from harm and they certainly do not want to see you get hurt. They are your cheerleading squad. They are in your corner and will cheer when you are winning; however, they do not have much in the locker that can help you when the chips are down. It is not that they do not want you to win in life but more so that they do not understand fully the game you are playing. Nonetheless, they will always be waiting in the wings to put their arm around you and tell you everything will be OK. They will help to dust you off; they will tell you what you want to hear, and that "maybe it just was not to be". They want to stay connected with you and as much as they want you to succeed, they do not want to lose you.

Your peer group are a like a specially selected crack commando unit that you have assembled. They are highly skilled, experienced and they understand the game you are playing. When you are winning, they are the people who keep you level headed and ensure you keep your focus. If you are losing, they have tactics, tools and techniques in their locker, which can get you back in the game quicker. Unlike your family and friends they will not just put their arm around you and listen to your excuses, they will hold you accountable and remind you just what you are capable of. They will nourish your mind, elevate your thinking and raise your standards. They are not afraid of seeing you move on to bigger and better things.

When I talk about friends in this context, I am talking about the kind of people who would take a bullet for you, unlike acquaintances or casual friends. I also accept that you may well have friends that form part of your peer group but for the sake of my illustration, I am generalizing.

So now, let me ask you again, which one would you choose to help you get back on track in a time of crisis?

I am guessing you would say peer group.

Now do not get me wrong, I am not saying that you should not turn to your family and friends at all. I am saying that if you want to bounce back and find your feet quickly, your peer group is going to help you achieve that more effectively.

During my business struggles, I could not really explain what was going on to my family, not because I did not want to, but because they probably would not understand. I had learnt to look at the world in a different way and had an unconventional business. They were supportive, they gave me love and they tried to stay positive, but they could see the pain in my eyes and they did not really know what to do.

It was my peer group that helped me get out of where I was. I got support, information and advice. They understood my plight very quickly and more significantly, focussed my mind on what I needed to do next. They did not allow me to wallow in self-pity or lose it completely. Instead, I was able to pull together a plan and they kept me accountable. I was not able to give them excuses and I found that just being around them, I felt sharper, stronger and more positive.

One of the best bits of advice I ever got was: "Love your family. Choose your peer group."

Principle #6 Change your route, not your destination.

When I was at school one of the most memorable phrases I can recall was "must try harder". I am sure some of you reading this book will be able resonate with that. It is an interesting phrase because it assumes that by trying harder and by doing the same thing; this will lead to a better result. Which is simply not true, yet we are conditioned to believe that is the case.

Einstein famously defined insanity as "doing the same thing over and over again and expecting different results", and yet often this is the approach that so many people use to solving problems. If business isn't working they just try harder, more hours doing more calls, more emails, more and more of the same thing in the hope that something different happens.

In physics there is a law called *The Law of Requisite Variety*, which says "the larger the variety of actions available to a control system, the larger the variety of perturbations it is able to compensate". In layman's terms, the greater your level of flexibility, the more options you can generate and therefore the greater the probability that you will achieve your goal.

When you are hit with a challenge or setback, you need to step back and look at not only what it is that you are doing but also more importantly, who it is you are being. By that, I mean what type of emotional energy are you giving off? People can smell fear and desperation a mile away. In my own experience, I recall when I was having a hard time moving the business forward, I just spent more and more hours trying the same strategies to get me enquires. The more I tried and failed the more desperate I felt on the inside, no matter how positive I thought I was being people could sense my plight. Not only that, but my decision-making was also infected with the same negative energy.

The last thing I wanted to do was to give up on my goals and my dreams but I knew I had to do something different. I kept saying I'd tried everything but in reality, however much I thought I'd exhausted all my options, there was always another...it just depended on how flexible I was willing to be without losing focus on my goal.

It is not about working harder, it is about being open to changing your approach as much or as many times as you need to in order for you to get to where you want. No matter how much you think that you have run out of choices, there are always other options for you to pursue.

Principle #7 Forgive and learn to let go.

Imagine you are driving along a busy road. What would happen if you kept your attention locked on the rear-view mirror so you could see what was behind you? The chances are you would probably end up crashing into something.

When things change, people have a tendency to hold on to the past for far too long. They become paralysed and unable to move on, using their past failings, shortcomings or mistakes as an excuse for not changing or taking that next step forward. They develop a signature story that they like to tell everyone they meet, to justify where they are and why they have been so unlucky in life.

The truth is the past is gone, it is behind you and there is nothing you can do to change it. The most powerful step you must take in order to move forward is to let go of what you are holding on to. Until you are prepared to let go of what you are holding on to; until you are willing to forgive yourself and others, you will not be able to move forward with conviction.

Here is the other thing you must appreciate about your past. Just because things may not have worked out how you expected them to last time, that does not mean the same will happen again.

The future has not happened yet, spending so much time and energy worrying about what might happen is just as paralysing as holding on to the past. The truth is that none of us can say for sure how the future will turn out. The only certainty about the future is that it will always be different from the past.

Let me be clear, I am not saying that you should forget the past; history has an important role to plan in your future. The most resourceful thing you can do with your past is to learn from it, pick out the golden nuggets of knowledge. Take the perspective of a student, asking: "What are the positive lessons I can take from the past that I can apply to my life, so that I can improve the results I am getting today?"

The most important place on your timeline is now – the present. If you dwell too much in the past or zoom too far ahead into the future, you will miss all the possibilities and opportunities, which will present themselves to you.

In the earlier example about driving whilst looking in the rear-view mirror, we agreed that the likelihood would be that you would crash. Equally, you would be in as much danger if you looked only straight ahead.

You do need to have the occasional glance in the mirror and focus on the path ahead, but in order to drive safely; you definitely need to be in the present. You need to be aware of what is happening around you so you can make changes; for instance, adjust your speed or change your lanes.

My motto for life has developed into: "Learn from the past, plan for the future, but live in the present."

I have only shared the tip of the iceberg in this introduction to the 7 principles. You can find out more by visiting my website www.vinayparmar.co.uk where you will find a range of resources to help you from training videos through to details of my live events. I hope that I can continue our relationship through these resources and that I am able to become part of your peer group to keep you in the best shape for bounce-back-ability.

I am not promising that by applying these principles you will suffer no further knock-backs in life, but what I can promise is that you will be better equipped to deal with them if and when those challenges arise.

Finally, I want to wish you well in your endeavours. I hope that life treats you well and that your challenges are not as severe or as tragic as some of mine have been. In writing this book, I have shared some of my inner deepest emotions and written from a place of honesty and integrity. Throughout each chapter there have been stages and accounts of my life that have brought me to the low-levels of despair – and as such the challenges that I have had to comes to terms with – the rewards have been sensational and life changing. I have experienced the dark times; I have questioned the hand that God dealt me; however, despite all the anxiety that I have endured, I persevered with the belief that I would achieve a life of fulfilment. My hope is that you, too, will be inspired to think differently about life, about change and about your ability to bounce back.

I would like to finish with a quote from one of my favorite speakers, Nido Qubein who says: "Not all change leads to improvement, but improvement is always the result of change."

Acknowledgements

On my journey I have been blessed to have met some amazing people who have, whether they know it or not, helped me to keep going and achieve what I have today.

This book is dedicated to parents - My Mom, Tara Parmar, you were taken from us too early but your star continues to shine brightly in our lives everyday. I love you and I miss you. Each day I strive to keep your spirit alive through my work and I carry your voice with me.

My Dad, Dhiraj Parmar, I love you. You are an inspiration to me in ways which you will never know. Thank you for always believing in me, especially when I didn't believe in myself.

To my Grandparents - I miss you all and I thank you for watching over me and continuing to be my guardian angels.

To my soul mate, best friend and the love of my life Jaymini, you simply complete me. Fate bought our hearts together and set us off on a journey which continues to fill me with more love for you each day. Thank you for being my rock, an amazing wife and the world's best mother.

To my ray of sunshine India, you will never fully know how much love, joy and bliss you have bought into my life. You represent hope, possibility and unconditional love - whatever the future holds I pray that you will continue to inspire those qualities in yourself and others.

There are no words I can think of to thank my incredible brother in law Atul and his wife Sheema. Your act of unconditional love, cleared the dark clouds on our horizon and allowed the sunlight to shine through.

To my loving family - Dipit and Rita, Ricky, Kaushika and my little champion Aaron, and my baby sister Ami - I love you all, thank you for all your support and encouragement.

To my dear mother-in-law Mrs Sushilaben Gohil - Thank you for always treating my like a son.

Thank you to my wonderful extended family - Amit and Kirti, Rakesh, Reekesh and Rashmi, Shantu Kaka and Surekha Kaki, Kanchan Foi and Uttam Fuwa, Sumi Foi, Dhaksaben and Vijay, Meenaben, Hemita, Mihir, Twinkle, Ketul, Hiten, Nitesh, and Maya.

To my Mom's wonderful sisters - Mina Masi, Pragna Masi, Aruna Masi and my marvelous Chandrika Mami - thank you for being my surrogate Moms and never letting me feel like I was without one - I love you all.

To my beloved Jayant Mama thank you for always having faith in me and my late Jitish Masa - though we spent only a few moments together your impact on me will last a lifetime.

To my musketeers - my amazing life long friends - Nilesh and Monique, Kam and Sonal, Bhavesh and Jo, Rita, Nina, Dipak and Meena - thank you for keeping me real and never allowing me to lose myself.

To my peer group, the crack commando unit, in my toughest of times you've always kept me grounded and never allowed me to let go of the dream - I will always appreciate that - Paul Harris, Robert Waghmare, Chris Williams, Elisabet Vinberg Hearn, Martin Astley and Jaz Binning.

To my extraordinary teachers - I may not have always learnt from you in person but you have helped shape my life and work - Tony Robbins, Toby and Kate McCartney, Martyn Wise, Topher Morrison, Steve and Dawn Siebold, Sanjay Shah, Dr Steven Covey, Zig Ziglar, Joel Roberts, Peter Senge, Tom Peters, David Taylor, Jim Rohn, Deepak Chopra, Benjamin Zander, Tracy Goss, Paul Wilde, and Joseph Campbell.

A huge thanks to all my supporters, promoters, and advocates - you guys rock!

Finally, a special thanks to the team that were key to the completion of this book:

To David Pilkington for being my guide, mentor and coach in writing this book .

To Lisa Barrett and Sian Lenegan from The Sixth Story for the being the creative geniuses that you are — thanks for the amazing book cover!

To Kathy De Mattia for helping me get my story out into the world - always remember you are amazing.

CPSIA information can be obtained at www.ICGtesting.com
Printed in the USA
BVOW012228230812

298714BV00001B/58/P